AMERICA'S SCHOOLS

The Battleground for Freedom

ALLEN QUIST

EdWatch

Chaska, Minnesota

America's Schools:
The Battleground for Freedom
Copyright ©2005 Allen Quist
All rights reserved

Cover Concept by Renee T. Doyle
Cover Design by Alpha Advertising
Interior Design by Pine Hill Graphics

Published by EdWatch
105 Peavey Road, Suite 116
Chaska, MN 55318
952-361-4931
http://www.edwatch.org
edwatch@lakes.com

ISBN: 0-9675196-4-0

Printed in the United States of America.

CONTENTS

Appendix

ACKNOWLEDGMENTS

This book is largely the product of EdWatch, a citizen group which exists for the purpose of promoting education policies that are academic, workable and consistent with the foundational principles of the United States. The organization includes Renee Doyle, President; Michael Chapman, researcher, writer and speaker; Dr. Karen Effrem, researcher, writer and speaker; and Julie Quist, my wife and Director of EdWatch, who contributed much of the research and most of the encouragement for the book.

In particular I would like to extend my thanks to Barbara Mattson, who did the proofreading and editing, and to Bonnie Gasper, who provided suggestions on overall organization and style. Thanks also to Minnesota State Senator Michele Bachmann and the many other state and federal legislators who have begun to take a stand for education policies that are good for our students and good for our country.

Allen Quist

PART I

The New Federal System of Education

CHAPTER ONE

The Battle of Our Time

In his Gettysburg Address, Abraham Lincoln said:

> Four score and seven years ago our fathers brought forth on this continent a new nation, conceived in Liberty, and dedicated to the proposition that all men are created equal. Now we are engaged in a great civil war, testing whether that nation, or any nation so conceived and so dedicated, can long endure.

Our nation is once again engaged in a great civil war. The issue is essentially the same as that stated by Lincoln—whether a nation conceived and born in liberty can long endure. The war is a war of ideas. The battle, however, could become much more than that. The Civil War and the Revolutionary War also began as battles of ideas. The issue once again is whether the United States will remain a free nation.

Where is this battle being fought? It is being waged in many areas of our nation, but one of the primary battle fronts is in the classrooms of our schools. A parent from Orem, Utah, for example, described the experience of her grade-school daughter as follows:

> Frustrated and confused, the tears swelling in her eyes needed no further explanation. Whereas she had been a high-achieving student in traditional math, she was now uncharacteristically reduced to tears from Connected Math's confused teaching approach.

This parent soon learned that her daughter was not alone. This parent soon learned that the frustration her daughter was experiencing in her math class was being repeated many thousands, perhaps millions, of times across our nation. This parent would soon learn that her daughter was one of the many casualties of the civil war of ideas now being waged in the United States of America.

Are all ideas equal? Are all moral systems equal? Are all cultures equal? They are not. History has shown that ideas do have consequences, and the damaging consequences can be so immense that they are virtually incomprehensible.

The Cold War was primarily a battle of ideas—about whether totalitarian Communism or the freedom of the West, led by the United States, would be the dominant force in the 21st Century. Totalitarian Communism has claimed the lives of over 100 million people in its brutal and failed attempts to achieve world dominance. Unimaginable suffering, beyond the deaths of the millions of innocents, is also part of the legacy of Communism's attempt to achieve world control.

The free world has been successful largely because it subscribes to the right ideas. The free world recognizes that some ideas are better than others. The free world also understands that nations can be taken over by forces of evil. At the same time, free countries know that the primary purpose of government is to protect its people and to subdue evil so that the God-given, inalienable rights of innocent people are protected.

What is the primary battle of ideas in our time? Hudson Institute scholar John Fonte has referred to this central battle as the "ideological civil war" (see Appendix A). It is a civil war of ideas, said Fonte, now taking place throughout the world and especially within the United States. This civil war, Fonte explained, is between those of us who believe that free nations, including the United States, should be preserved as free and sovereign states versus those seeking to transform America and the world into something radically different.

This battle of ideas is the central battle being waged in our schools. It is taking place not only in our public schools, but in private and home schools as well. This battle involves the purpose of education as well as the definition of what education should be.

The new transformational purpose of education was described by Dr. Shirley McCune, one of the featured speakers at the 1989 National Governor's Conference, the conference that recommended Goals 2000 to the nation. (She was also one of the top executives at McREL—an agency set up to implement Goals 2000 in the states.) In her article "Transforming Education," McCune described the agenda of those like herself who wish to make radical changes in America. She described the desired changes as follows:

> Our society has undergone profound economic, demographic, and social transformation—a transformation that

impacts virtually every aspect of our individual and collective lives. It is the manifestation of a new era of civilization…and the movement from a national to a global society. Virtually every institution is forced to restructure to meet a changed environment and changed needs. [Shirley McCune, *Creating The Future* (Seattle: New Horizons for Learning, 1998), http://www.newhorizens.org]

The word "transformation," as used by McCune and others, captures the central theme promoted by those seeking the radical makeover of our country. These intellectuals intend to discard what has been the United States of America. They intend to then construct a totally different America based on their worldview.

Most Americans are opposed to this transformation. John Fonte described the conflict over the planned transformation as follows:

Beneath the surface of American politics an intense ideological struggle is being waged between two competing worldviews. [The traditional view favors] the transmission of the American regime, the other camp [favors] its transformation. [John Fonte, *Policy Review*, December 2000, pp. 15 & 31]

(John Fonte worked with Lynn Cheney, wife of Vice-President Dick Cheney, in opposing the National History Standards. The U.S. Senate voted against these History Standards by a margin of 99 to 1. The U.S. Department of Education, under then President Clinton, implemented the History Standards anyway after cosmetic changes were made.)

A recent issue of *Time* magazine called the people behind the planned transformation of our country the "new millennialists." *Time* described these individuals as follows:

[The new millennialists] believe that America is not just on the verge of transformation, but duty bound to create it. [*Time*, December 8, 2003, p. 82]

McCune and other supporters of our nation's transformation believe that now is the time to create what she called a "new era of civilization." This will be a new age, she says, that is the "movement from a national to a global society." Virtually every institution, she insists, must "restructure" to accommodate this new globalist age. What institutions does she believe must now restructure? As we shall see in subsequent chapters, they include (1) government, (2) education, (3) business, (4) churches, and (5) the family.

These radicals believe we must also restructure our view of knowledge—nothing will be viewed as true any more because, they say, there is no such thing as real truth. They apply evolution broadly to include the world of ideas. Old ideas must be inferior, they believe, simply because they are old. New ideas, similarly, must be superior simply because they are new. Nothing, to them, however, can be said to be true.

Morality and human rights are also redefined by this postmodernist worldview. Nothing is viewed as being morally right or wrong of its own accord. Human rights are seen as evolving just as everything else evolves. Individual property rights may have seemed right for people of the past, for example, but private property rights are viewed as obsolete today. Similarly, the taking of innocent human life may have been wrong in the past, but, as the radicals see it, then was then, and now is now. Something having been wrong in the past does not make it wrong today. Indeed, prominent ethical philosopher Peter Singer says that preferring the preservation of human life over other forms of life is indefensible because every form of life has an equal right to its preservation.

The transformation of America is also being accomplished by our courts. Legal scholar Robert Bork described the U.S. Supreme Court as follows:

> Most members of the [Supreme] Court belong to...an intellectual elite that believes it enjoys superior enlightenment and that its business is to spread this benefit to those living on the lower slopes of human achievement. Hence the steady stream of Court decisions striking down various restrictions on abortion, of the telecasting of sex acts, and on computer simulated child pornography and outlawing any aspect of religion even remotely bearing on government. [These are the same justices, said Bork, who now reference court decisions in other countries in order to defend their own decisions.] [Robert Bork, "Whose Constitution Is It, Anyway?" *National Review*, December 8, 2003, p.37]

The American public doesn't support such Court rulings, however. That doesn't matter to the elitists because they believe that the enlightened intellectuals of this new age know better than the public. The way they see it, the enlightened intellectuals will make the decisions for the unenlightened masses.

How are the new change-agents hoping to bring about this transformation of America? They recognize that doing so requires that they take control of our American system of education. They began with the public schools, but they are having increasing success with private schools and home schools as well.

The utopians view education quite differently than do other Americans. The two opposing views of education were accurately described by Katherine Kersten, scholar at Minnesota's Center of the American Experiment, when she said:

> Most Americans see the public school as an institution dedicated to the transmission of knowledge.... [Others] view it as something quite different: an agent of radical social change. [*Star Tribune*, November 9, 2003]

The issue is academic, knowledge-based education versus radical, transformational education. Traditional academic education is committed to teaching knowledge. Academic education believes in the foundational principles of the United States. Academic education is committed to teaching these fundamental principles of freedom to our children.

Transformational education, in contrast, rejects all the objectives stated above. Transformational education is committed to changing America, not preserving it. The change-agents know that America is not going to be transformed by knowledge-based education. America can only be radically transformed by an education system that focuses on changing the attitudes, values, behavior and worldview of its students. This is the kind of education the transformers have created. To do so, however, they first had to take control of the schools.

The following chapters will explain how the radicals have largely succeeded in taking over our schools. The story begins with the subject area one might expect to be the least controversial of all—that of mathematics. The reader may, however, have some familiarity with the "math wars" of the past several years. As will be demonstrated, these math wars are a consequence of the civil war of ideas. The math wars are one front in the battle between those who believe in academic education versus those who subscribe to transformational education.

The question is this: Do our schools exist to educate the child and to transmit our culture, or do schools exist for the purpose of making our children into political activists on behalf of a new and radical vision of what the elitists believe our country should be? The drama begins with integrated math.

CHAPTER TWO

Integrated Math

One would not expect the field of mathematics to provide a battle-ground for the war of ideas. That is why this book begins with mathematics. Understanding what is happening in math education provides a window for understanding what is happening in all of education. Indeed, the transformation of math education is a microcosm of the changes in all of education. We begin with an overview of integrated math.

Integrated math takes a variety of forms. Integrated math includes "Core Plus," "Chicago Math," "Investigations," "Foundations," "Connected Math," "NCEE Math," "Everyday Math," "Contemporary Math" and many others. Integrated math is also referred to as "new math," "fuzzy math," "whole math," "constructivist math" and "standards-based math." Integrated math is based on the National Math Standards (Federal Curriculum) also called "NCTM" standards, which were written in 1989 and revised in 2000. NCTM is the acronym for the National Council of Teachers of Mathematics. Integrated math to a lesser degree is based on recommendations made by the U.S. Department of Education in 1999.

Integrated math is "integrated" in three ways: (1) Traditionally separate subject areas, such as algebra and geometry, are combined into one course of study. The two subjects are integrated. (2) Math principles are taught as applied to current social or political issues such as environmentalism. Mathematics and the politically-correct worldview are integrated. (The national curriculum standards for civics and government require that the new civics, including environmentalism, be taught in all subjects including math. In addition, the National Council for Social Studies recommends that multiculturalism be integrated into all subject areas, including math.) (3) Math principles are taught in the context of a student's supposed real-world personal experiences. Mathematics and the student's life are integrated.

These three modes of math integration are described in the math standards for the State of Washington which read as follows:

> The student understands how mathematical ideas connect within mathematics, other subject areas, and real-life situations. [p. 33 of the Washington Education Standards]

That is, math is integrated (1) within math, (2) with other subjects, and (3) with the life of the student.

Integrated math includes several controversial approaches to teaching. These pedagogical strategies include:

1. **Discovery learning.** Students are expected to figure out or design mathematical formulas and principles on their own.
2. **Group projects.** Students do math problems in groups instead of individually.
3. **Non-directed learning**, also called "student-centered" learning. Teachers become "facilitators" instead of being "instructors."
4. **Reliance on calculators.** Students use calculators, even in the lower grades, and not much arithmetic is learned. The drill exercises in traditional math are discouraged. Students also use calculators on achievement tests. The new SAT test, for example, will allow students to use calculators while taking the test.

These teaching strategies, along with mandates for teaching the themes of civics, environmentalism, population growth, multiculturalism and the like in math classes, have the net effect of reducing the time available for actually teaching mathematics. Time on task for the actual learning of mathematics is substantially reduced. As a consequence, major areas of the logical sequences in math education are either minimized or omitted altogether.

In spite of its major shortcomings, however, integrated math received a huge boost in 1999 when the U.S. Department of Education recommended five different integrated math programs as "exemplary" and five others as being "promising." Over 200 mathematicians and scientists, including four Nobel Prize winners, were so outraged over the Department's recommendations that they took out an ad in the *Washington Times* (11/18/99) protesting the actions and asking Secretary of Education Richard Riley to withdraw the recommendations. The Department refused to withdraw the recommendations, however, and many of the schools who have switched over to integrated math have done so, in part, because of the Department of Education's recommendations supporting integrated math.

The recommendations of the Department were vulnerable to criticism on numerous grounds—one of them being that only one member of the "Experts Panel" which made the recommendations has a Ph.D. in mathematics. This individual either voted "No" or abstained in all of the Department's recommendations. [e-mail letter from Dr. R. James Milgram, Professor of Mathematics at Stanford University, forwarded to EdWatch.org, October 31, 2000]

The net effect of integrated math is that student achievement in math drops through the floor once schools adopt the new program. Students schooled in the new math understandably have difficulty succeeding in college. Dr. Lawrence Gray, Director of Undergraduate Studies in the School of Mathematics at the University of Minnesota, made this report:

> In a study of 150 college math students, 60 did not continue with their classes in later semesters. Thirty of those did not have enough high school math courses to prepare them for college math. However, the other 30 were not able to understand the material taught in the classes. Two of those students came from traditional math programs, and 28 of those students came from integrated math programs like Core-Plus. [Reported in the Fairmont *Sentinel* newspaper, March 9, 2001]

Dr. Gray also said that on math placement tests at the University of Minnesota, students who have taken integrated math score at significantly lower levels than students who have taken traditional math. [*Ibid.*]

Dr. R. James Milgram, Professor of Mathematics at Stanford University, made similar observations when he said:

> Connected math…is filled with major mathematical errors and misconceptions. Moreover, it is aimed at roughly the lowest quartile of a typical class, rather than the middle. Consequently, the material contained is generally one to two years below grade level…. As to Core-Plus, it recently became the mandated program in all the high schools in Milwaukee. But the University of Wisconsin at Madison won't accept it as satisfying the mathematics entry requirement. [From an e-mail message from Dr. Milgram forwarded to EdWatch.org, October 31, 2000]

Dr. Fred Greenleaf, Professor of Mathematics at New York University, commented on New York City's recent adoption of integrated math as follows:

> I had no idea just how bad the NCTM-based math programs being introduced in the city really were.... It is clear to us [now, however,] that the NCTM programs, if they remain in place, are going to have a terrifically negative impact on the prospects of all students who aspire to college. [paper delivered to the National Association of Scholars Convention, May 22, 2004, p. 1]

Because of steadily declining test scores, the Regents of California's public schools tossed out integrated math in 1997. Since discarding integrated math, the math test scores of California's K-12 students have shown dramatic improvement (*Ibid.* p. 4). California had adopted integrated math five years earlier.

The scholarly Fordham Foundation reported that the National Science Foundation has spent $1 billion over the past five years promoting integrated math. This obscene abuse of taxpayer money prompted the Fordham Foundation to issue the following statement:

> No single institution in the United States has caused more damage to the mathematical education of our children than...the National Science Foundation. [David Klein, *The Education Gadfly*, (publication of the Fordham Foundation) March 4, 2004]

In spite of the defective nature of integrated math, the textbook companies use the status of the National Science Foundation to market their integrated math textbooks. The 2004 McGraw-Hill catalog, for example, states:

> **Research-Based and Classroom-Tested.** Developed with funding from **National Science Foundation,** each course in *Contemporary Mathematics In Context* is the product of a four-year research, development, and evaluation process involving thousands of students in schools across the country. [p. 34]

A sales representative of McGraw-Hill told the author privately that the company knows that integrated math is inferior to traditional math, but the company carries it anyway, he said, because some schools want it. (As is evident from the quotation above, the terms "research-based" and "class-room tested" are meaningless terms in education. These terms are used, however, for the promotion of products, many of which are inferior to other offerings.)

Dramatically declining test scores have obviously been one of the biggest obstacles for integrated math. That barrier, however, is in the process of being minimized by the federal education system. That is, the national tests are now being rewritten to conform to the NCTM standards, and that means conformity to integrated math. How successful this will be is difficult to say, but under the new tests those students who have been schooled in integrated math will score higher than they would on valid tests because the tests have been rewritten to conform to the integrated system. At the same time, we now have no way of knowing what the scores on the new tests actually mean.

The federal government itself has one test that it uses to measure academic achievement in the various states. That test is called the NAEP (National Assessment Educational Progress), also called the "Nation's Report Card." Under the No Child Left Behind federal law, all states are now required to administer this test. This NAEP test has already been rewritten to conform to the NCTM integrated math system. The writers of the NAEP described how this has been the goal all along when they said:

> The national standards should drive the NAEP. The National Assessment Governing Board's apparent willingness to do so is visible in its efforts to alter NAEP to incorporate NCTM standards as they have emerged since 1988. [*National Education Goals Panel Report*, January 24, 1992, p. 7]

Similarly, the Stanford achievement test web page says that its tests, also, are now based on the national standards (Federal Curriculum) which include integrated math. The new SAT will similarly be based on the national standards. In other words, we are now experiencing plummeting student achievement in mathematics, as occurred previously in California, but that disaster is not showing up on national tests because the tests have been restructured to follow the same content as the national standards. It is like the old joke about the fisherman with a rubber ruler—the fish may have been smaller than he said, but the ruler was able to adjust just enough to fit any size fish.

Why is this happening? Why would our nation's education system adopt an unproven approach to teaching mathematics that is having disastrous results? It sounds almost too crazy to be true. Why would anyone do something this destructive to our children? And how can anyone have enough influence to make these changes?

THE IMPACT OF FEDERAL LAW

All fifty states signed on to the 1994 federal law known as the Goals 2000: Educate America Act. The states did so, not because they viewed the federal programs being beneficial, but because they learned they would lose all federal education money if they did not join. When states joined, they were required to accept all eight federal education goals as stipulated by Goals 2000. Goal three of Goals 2000 says:

> **GOAL 3: Student Achievement and Citizenship.** By the year 2000, all students will leave grades 4, 8 and 12 having demonstrated competency over challenging subject matter including English, mathematics, science, foreign languages, civics and government, economics, arts, history, and geography....

Notice the words "all" students and "competency over challenging subject matter." In Goals 2000, "all" students meant all students—100% of the students. What percentage of twelfth grade students would demonstrate "competency in challenging subject matter" in mathematics today? Far less than 100% of twelfth graders would meet this standard. As a result, Goals 2000 forced our education program to focus its efforts on the lowest achieving students. Average and gifted students already meet the standard. The lowest achieving students are the ones targeted by the law at the expense of the average and superior students.

Some schools have adopted integrated math thinking that it would help these low achieving students. Will that actually happen? The Fordham Foundation believes it will actually harm them. Fordham said:

> Fuzzy math programs cause problems for all children, but they are especially harmful to children with limited resources. Upper middle class parents can afford tutoring...lower income children typically do not have that option. [David Klein, *The Education Gadfly*, March 4, 2004]

And, Dr. Fred Greenleaf said:

> Students whose parents are not affluent enough to afford extensive tutoring in the middle-school and high school years are simply out of luck. [paper delivered to the National Association of Scholars Convention, p. 1, May 22, 2004]

Since the NCTM math standards are part of the entire federal education system, these standards were also targeted toward the low achieving students. That is one reason why the standards are dumbed down and restructured. The standards were not developed to be good for the majority of students. They were focused on the lowest achievers. Unfortunately, however, the effect has been that the NCTM standards are detrimental for all students and are especially detrimental to low-income students.

This bad situation has become even worse under the federal No Child Left Behind (NCLB) act signed into law in 2002. NCLB requires states to first reduce, and then eliminate, all disparities in academic performance in math and language arts which are identifiable by racial, ethnic or socio-economic group. NCLB mandates that all states give yearly achievement tests to all public school students in grades 3 through 8, and at least once in grades 9 through 12. States are then required to show "adequate yearly progress" (AYP) on a variety of measures including a reduction of disparities identified on the basis of race, ethnicity and socio-economic group. By the year 2014, NCLB requires that states "close the achievement gaps" which have been identified. NCLB also requires states to bring all students up to specified proficiency levels by that time.

Specifically NCLB requires that:

> ...states must describe how they will close the achievement gap and make sure all students, including those who are disadvantaged, achieve academic proficiency. [Executive Summary of NCLB]

No Child Left Behind requires all states to adopt state standards in mathematics and other areas. In addition, states are required to base their student achievement tests on their state standards. Many states and schools have concluded that the path of least resistance is to simply adopt integrated math standards since that is what the federal government will be testing their schools on anyway.

If schools do not demonstrate "adequate yearly progress" in meeting their goals, they are subject to a variety of sanctions, including being identified as failing schools, and they ultimately can be taken over by the state if they cannot comply. Once again federal law forces schools to target the lowest achieving students in its math programs, now with real teeth in the law. All the while, student progress will ultimately be measured by the NAEP test which is based on integrated math.

The education planners have created a spider's web of integrated math that impacts state schools from all directions. As a result, math curriculum decisions are too often based on money, self-preservation, and status—not on what is good for our children and certainly not on what is best for our nation.

THE IMPACT OF IDEOLOGY

Federal laws, however, only begin to explain why integrated math is being forced upon our schools. The federal laws are themselves the product of philosophical points of view. That is, the federal laws in question, as well as the new math itself, are primarily driven by ideology. The issue is largely the battle of ideas. Ideas do have consequences, and sometimes the consequences are profound.

Why, for example, do some minority groups (but not all) score consistently lower than whites on math proficiency tests? The most likely explanation can be found in the research of Barbara Dafoe Whitehead. Whitehead has concluded that there is a powerful correlation between intact families and success of children on a wide range of measures including school performance. Whitehead's research suggests that racial and ethnic differences in achievement tests are primarily the result of family structure, not race. If you adjust for family structure, says Whitehead, the racial and ethnic differences largely disappear. [Barbara Dafoe Whitehead, "Dan Quayle Was Right," *Atlantic*, April, 1993] Unless No Child Left Behind has a way of rebuilding families (it doesn't), it is avoiding the real reason for disparities in student achievement.

In spite of such difficulties, there are approaches to education that have been very successful in raising the performance of all students, including members of minorities. Direct Instruction, for example, has succeeded in raising the math and reading abilities of inner city minority students to levels far higher than their white, suburban counterparts. Core Knowledge has demonstrated similar results. Traditional mathematics, taught well, is also successful. Education expert E. D. Hirsch says that the best way to raise the performance of all students is to abandon progressive education and return to traditional education because that is what really works. (The education strategies that work are designed to raise the achievement of all students, not just the low achievers.)

The education change-agents, however, do not like traditional education because they want to transform America, not preserve it. They reject the thesis that intact, two-parent families are superior to other options. As a consequence, the designers of the new education system look elsewhere for an explanation and for solutions for poor math performance, especially among minorities. Where do the designers look?

POSTMODERNISM

Postmodernism is the dominant ideology behind integrated math. Postmodernism believes that knowledge and truth are really just thought-forms known as "constructs." Postmodernists believe that the language and other paradigms of the dominant culture (such as mathematics) are devised to keep other cultures and subcultures in positions of inferiority. (See Chapter 3.)

Jack Price, former NCTM President, put it this way: "[Traditional math is] good for high socioeconomic-status white males." [KidsDoCount, *http://snow.prohosting.com/mathiq*] Price's statement means that math is allegedly a construct of powerful white males and is used to keep all others in positions of inferiority. That is standard postmodernist dogma.

An article written by Marilyn Strutchens, printed in ERIC Digest, published by the U.S. Department of Education, describes the worldview which she says forms the foundation for NCTM math. (Marilyn Strutchens' husband helped design integrated math with funding from the National Science Foundation.) The article by Strutchens, which is sympathetic to integrated math, is called, "Multicultural Mathematics: A More Inclusive Mathematics." The article explained what Strutchens believes is the real nature of NCTM math. She said:

> NCTM math...provide[s] a framework for empowering all of our students through multicultural mathematics. [Marilyn Strutchens, "Multicultural Mathematics: A More Inclusive Mathematics," ERIC Clearinghouse for Science, Mathematics and Environmental Education, p. 2]

In using the term "multicultural mathematics," Strutchens is really describing postmodern mathematics. "Empowering students" is a central concept in postmodernism. [As David Horowitz observes, "multiculturalism" also describes the worldview of Marxist writer Antonio Gramsci. (See Chapter 4.)] Strutchens further explained her observations by saying that NCTM math is "multicultural...in order to make higher level mathematics accessible to all students." [*Ibid.*] She sees traditional math as a filter for keeping minorities and women in lower levels of achievement and employment. Integrated math is supposed to remove that filter. All students can learn math equally, says Strutchens, by escaping from what she calls "Eurocentric mathematics." The underlying assumption here is the postmodernist viewpoint that math is a construct, not a matter of truth, and is different for various cultures and races.

The Minneapolis *Star Tribune* (2/19/04) quoted psychologist JoAnn Deak on the issue of integrated math. Deak is a researcher specializing in differences between boys and girls. Deak said that the brains of boys and girls are somewhat different when it comes to mathematics (as is well known). In her recommendations, she said: "Different teaching approaches early in a child's life can make up for these gender differences." In other words, traditional math is supposedly "male math," and we should also be teaching "female math" so that boys and girls can be equal in math. This feminist viewpoint is another central element in postmodern math.

As is evident from the quotations above, the motivating force behind integrated math is ideological, not pedagogical (effective instruction). Integrated math is postmodern math. Since postmodernism is a false worldview, its application to education can only be destructive. As will be seen in later chapters, the application of postmodernism to other subject areas, where it takes the form of revisionist history and the new civics, is equally destructive.

Postmodernism not only shapes the content of integrated math, it also shapes its methodology. Why, for example, does integrated math prefer group projects over individual learning? It is because postmodernists reject individualism in favor of group identity (collectivism). The group projects are not intended to improve academic performance. They are all about changing the child's view of what it means to be a person. In addition, the message of group projects is that the well-being of the group is more important than the well-being or rights of the individual—more postmodernist ideology.

Why does integrated math include a heavy emphasis on discovery learning? (Discovery learning is known to be an inefficient way to learn academic subjects.) The reason postmodernists stress discovery learning is because they believe that traditional math is not true; that math is not part of a real world outside of one's mind. Discovery learning is intended to weaken the concept that truth exists outside the experience of the student. Discovery learning, under the guidance of the proper teacher, is also seen as being an essential part of transformational education. (See Chapter 4.)

Why does integrated math include a reliance on calculators as opposed to learning arithmetic? It is because postmodernists believe that math is a construct, not reality. What, then, is the point of learning arithmetic? The original NCSS standards actually said that learning arithmetic could be harmful to children. Why? As we will see in subsequent chapters, postmodernists view arithmetic as a construct used by the powerful to subdue the weak. As they see it, the less arithmetic children learn, the better. In addition, memorizing multiplication tables implies that the tables are real and true—postmodernists do not want students to think that way.

The same principles hold true for the redefinition of teachers as "facilitators" instead of as "instructors." Postmodernists view teachers as being instruments of power, agents of the oppressor class; not as individuals with legitimate authority who are actually helping students by conveying real knowledge, real truth and real morality to them. (See Chapters 3 and 4.)

EVOLUTION

The new and expanded approach to Darwinism provides another component to the ideological foundation for integrated math. A recent issue of the Minneapolis *Star Tribune* quoted researcher David Geary, Professor of Psychology at the University of Missouri, who believes that evolution explains the poor performance in mathematics by some students. Geary said, "the human brain is not designed to accept math easily." He also said:

> Much of what kids are expected to learn has been developed in the past 1,000 to 2,000 years, and thus people's brains aren't really designed to learn much of it...[*Star Tribune*, 2-19-04]

In other words, according to Geary, math education is foreign to the brains of most children. The implication is that math must be redesigned to be more user-friendly and more relevant to the personal lives of students (more integrated). In addition, many advocates of the new and overly broad view of evolution assume that new methods will be superior to old methods simply because they are new. They don't need any studies to tell them what they are already convinced must be true.

CONSTRUCTIVISM

Education researchers of KidsDoCount correctly define "constructivism" as follows:

> The new math programs embraced the progressive learning philosophy called "constructivism," the mental processes of abstraction and reflection followed by learning. This means that students are somehow to construct their own knowledge-base of mathematical laws, formulas, and algorithms by

self-teaching. The vague hope is that kids can do this partly by inventing their own techniques through extensive hands-on exploration (discovery), but with little help or explanations from the teacher.... Furthermore, to accommodate the kids inventing their own techniques, the mathematics has been necessarily "watered down." [http://snow.prohosting.com/mathiq]

Marilyn Strutchens agrees that constructivism is the underlying philosophy of the NCTM math standards. She said that constructivist education requires that:

Teachers see themselves as facilitators helping students to construct their own knowledge of mathematics. Teachers encourage students to learn collaboratively, students are expected to teach each other and be responsible for each other. The validation of student-invented algorithms is important for self-esteem and belief in their ability to do mathematics. Teachers can help students see that mathematics is derived from real-life situations by exposing them to ethnomathematics practiced among identifiable cultural groups, such as national-tribal societies, labor groups, children of certain age brackets, professional classes, and so on. [Marilyn Strutchens, "Multicultural Mathematics: A More Inclusive Mathematics," ERIC Clearinghouse for Science, Mathematics and Environmental Education, pp. 3-4]

Constructivism assumes that knowledge is always changing and is, therefore, of little importance. Constructivists are more interested in processes, like "thinking mathematically," than in content, like "understanding mathematics."

There are different kinds of constructivism. One type, known as "radical constructivism," has the same meaning as postmodernism. The definitions are identical. When Marilyn Strutchens, as explained above, says that integrated math is an application of constructivism, she is using the definition of radical constructivism. In other words, saying that integrated math is constructivist math—a conclusion that everyone in the field seems to support—is just another way of saying that integrated math is postmodern math.

This is the recipe for the new math: Start with traditional mathematics, then infuse it with postmodernism; use critical class time to teach civics, environmentalism and multiculturalism; devise different teaching methods for different races and for boys versus girls; mix it thoroughly with expanded evolutionary theory; make teachers into facilitators instead of instructors; require group learning; use the better students to tutor the slow learners; minimize or remove key building blocks in the math sequences; dumb it down by one or two grade levels; and then have students invent their own math because it is supposedly good for their self-esteem. Add a shot of utopianism, and then target all the education strategies toward the lowest achieving students. No wonder NCTM math is such a disaster!

The new math is something like this. It is like a bald eagle that was soaring along fairly well until the federal government and its ideologues decided to strap a dozen ten-pound bricks to its back. This bird is not going to fly.

The new math is being forced on our schools—not because it will improve math performance. There are no reliable tests which show that integrated math actually works. There are numerous studies which reveal that it doesn't. Integrated math is being forced on our schools because of radical ideology. It is the ideology of the new Federal Curriculum. It is the utopian worldview of the self-appointed change-agents who believe they have been chosen to transform our people and our land into their vision of the brave new world.

(For an excellent study of methods that really work in raising academic achievement of minority and inner city children, see *No Excuses: Seven principles of Low Income Schools Who Set the Standard for High Achievement*, the Heritage Foundation, www.noexcuses.org)

(For a description of how Kipp Academy raises student achievement of inner city children to levels far above their suburban counterparts, see *U. S. News and World Report*, March 17, 2004.)

CHAPTER THREE

Postmodernism

As was noted in Chapter 2, postmodernism provides much of the philosophical base for the federal education system. Integrated math, for example, as we have seen, is really postmodern math. This chapter describes postmodernism in more detail.

Gene Edward Veith's classic work, *Postmodern Times*, says that postmodernism consists of the following positions:

(1) *Social Constructivism.* Meaning, morality, and truth do not exist objectively; rather, they are constructed by the society.

(2) *Cultural Determinism.* Individuals are wholly shaped by the cultural forces. Language in particular determines what we can think, trapping us in a "prison-house of language."

(3) *The Rejection of Individual Identity.* People exist primarily as members of groups. The phenomenon of American individualism is itself a construction of American culture with its middle-class values of independence and introspection, but it remains an illusion. Identity is primarily collective.

(4) *The Rejection of Humanism.* Values that emphasize the creativity, autonomy, and priority of human beings are misplaced. There is no universal humanity since every culture constitutes its own reality. Traditional humanistic values are canons of exclusion, oppression, and crimes against the natural environment. Groups must empower themselves to assert their own values and to take their place with other planetary species.

(5) *The Denial of the Transcendent.* There are no absolutes. Even if there were, we would have no access to them since we are bound to our culture and imprisoned in our language.

(6) *Power Reductionism.* All institutions, all human relationships, all moral values, and all human creations—from works of art to religious ideologies—are all expressions of the primal will to power.

(7) *The Rejection of Reason.* Reason and the impulse to objectify truth are illusory masks for cultural power. Authenticity and fulfillment come from submerging the self into a larger group, releasing one's natural impulses such as honest emotions and sexuality, cultivating subjectivity, and developing a radical openness to existence by refusing to impose order on one's life.

(8) *Revolutionary Critique of the Existing Order.* Modern society with its rationalism, order, and unitary view of truth needs to be replaced with a new world order. Scientific knowledge reflects an outdated modernism, though the new electronic technology holds great promise. Segmentation of society into its constituent groups will allow for a true cultural pluralism. The old order must be swept away, to be replaced by a new, as yet unclearly defined, mode of communal existence. [Gene Edward Veith Jr. *Postmodern Times: A Christian Guide to Contemporary Thought and Culture* (Wheaton: Crossways Books, 1994), pp. 158-159]

Veith also says: "The belief that reality is socially constructed, as David Horowitz has pointed out, can only be a formula for totalitarianism." [*Ibid.* p. 159] Postmodernism is a false view of reality. For that reason, we should not be surprised that postmodernism is destructive to genuine learning—as is so clearly illustrated by the total failure of integrated math.

CHAPTER FOUR

Antonio Gramsci

S ocialism, in the classical sense, is virtually dead among the intellectual elites of the United States. Traditional Communism, similarly,
now has few followers in America. Marxism, however, is alive and
well. It is the new form of Marxism—that variety formulated by Italian
Marxist Antonio Gramsci that is now enthusiastically embraced by many
members of the American intelligentsia, especially by those in the colleges and universities of our nation. As David Horowitz has said, "The
mentality is Stalinist, but it is the particular Stalinism of Antonio Gramsci
that informs the multicultural fervor in the academy." According to
Horowitz, Gramsci is now the intellectual mentor of the postmodern left.
[David Horowitz, "Up From Multiculturalism," January, 1998, p. 1.
http://www.fiuedu/~yaf/multigarbage.html see Appendix C.]

Former President Bill Clinton is a fan of Antonio Gramsci (pro-
nounced "gram-she"). Clinton studied Gramsci when he was a student
in Europe (while he was dodging the draft). Gramsci has been
described as "Clinton's ideological guru" while he was at Oxford. [Tal
Brooke, *One World* (Berkeley: End Run Publishing, 2000), p. 109]

Antonio Gramsci (1891-1937) agreed with Karl Marx in advocating
a new world order where there would supposedly be no class distinctions. Gramsci also agreed with Marx that the fundamental cause of
misery in the world is the exploitation of the poor and vulnerable by
those who are strong and who control the world. Gramsci disagreed
with Marx, however, on the basic dynamic by which the powerful supposedly exploit everyone else.

Marx said that the cause of this exploitation is economic. According
to Marx, if a country eliminated private ownership of property and
installed collective ownership (socialism) instead, the tyranny of the
rich over the poor would be ended. Today's Marxists, however, have

largely concluded that socialism does not work. The march of Communist China away from socialism to a mixture of market economics and centralized planning is clearly a case in point.

Gramsci disagreed with Marx's position that economics is the fundamental dynamic by which the powerful subjugate everyone else. The basic cause of exploitation, said Gramsci, is cultural, not economic. The powerful remain in control, wrote Gramsci, by controlling the culture—that is, by controlling the language and other thought-forms that constitute the culture.

A country's economic system, said Gramsci, is the result of the culture, not its cause. This is why, he said, the West has been unwilling to embrace Marxism. Gramsci said that the only way to break up the ruling elite in the West is by changing its way of speaking and its way of thinking—by changing its culture.

How then can one change the culture of the West? According to Gramsci, the primary way to change a nation's culture is by changing its system of education. Gramsci called this "transformational education." Transformational education is that system of education also called for in the Earth Charter, by the Agenda 21 Action Plan of the Earth Summit and by Dr. Shirley McCune who helped design the Federal Curriculum. Transformational education is focused on changing the worldview of the child, not on academic education.

In his paper "On Education," Antonio Gramsci said that transformational education must accomplish the following goals [www.marxists.org/archive/gramsci]:

(1) Deconstruct the language of education, including that of history, civics, mathematics and science. Like the postmodernists, Gramsci said that language, history, mathematics and other academic disciplines are not "truths," they are "constructs"—mental images used by the powerful to subdue the vulnerable. For that reason, said Gramsci, these languages must be "deconstructed." In the new Federal Curriculum, the Gramsci-style deconstruction and reconstruction takes the form of integrated math, revisionist history, the National Council for Social Studies (NCSS) canon for language arts, the new civics, etc. The national *Curriculum Standards for the Social Studies* follow the Gramsci paradigm when it describes its goals for students as follows:

> Knowing how to read and reconstruct the past allows one to develop a historical perspective and to answer questions such as: Who am I? What happened in the past, etc.? [*Curriculum Standards for the Social Studies*, Maryland, National Council for Social Studies, 1994, p. x]

And:

> Knowledge is contracted by learners as they attempt to fit new information, experiences, feelings, and relationships into their existing or emerging intellectual, aesthetic, and emotional constructs. [*Ibid.* p. 7]

As is apparent from the quotations above, the national *Curriculum Standards for the Social Studies* (Federal Curriculum) is based on the ideological framework of Antonio Gramsci. (The NCSS has also been aggressively promoting multiculturalism. Multiculturalism is based on the theory of Antonio Gramsci. (See Chapter 5.) This federal curriculum is intended to transform the lives of our students along the lines Gramsci recommended.

(2) Emphasize discovery learning. Gramsci said that escaping from the constructs of the powerful requires that students must avoid the instruction of teachers and textbooks and must discover truth on their own. Said Gramsci:

> It [the Gramsci school] indicates that learning takes place especially through a spontaneous and autonomous effort of the pupil with the teacher only exercising a function of friendly guide. [Antonio Gramsci, "On Education," p. 8]

The reader may be aware of the new role of teachers in the federal education system, that of being "guide on the side" instead of "sage on the stage." This new view of teachers and learning was articulated by Antonio Gramsci. It is the view of education promoted by all the national standards, including the integrated math (NCTM) standards. Discovery learning is known as being an inefficient method of instruction (see the writings of E. D. Hirsch), but academic achievement is not the goal of the international education system. The goal of international education is transforming our children to supposedly escape from the constructs of the past and to become political activists on behalf of the new world order.

(3) Focus on group projects. The reader will recall the emphasis on discovery learning and group projects which are integral to integrated math (see Chapter 2). Group projects are also emphasized in all subject areas of the new federal education system. Why are group projects important to the new system? Gramsci said that group learning is necessary to develop "mass consciousness" and "revolutionary consciousness." Students must learn in groups, said Gramsci, so they will see themselves as part of the group, not as individuals. Group projects are also necessary, he said, to change the values, attitudes and worldview of the student.

Gramsci called this process of using group projects "consciousness transformation." Gramsci additionally said that students must be "active participants" in the education process if they are to change. Discovery learning and group projects are both designed to makes students active participants. The over-emphasis in the new education system on group projects follows the recommendations of Antonio Gramsci.

(4) Eliminate the two-track system of education. Gramsci said that the two-track system of education (college-bound versus vocational) exists for the sole purpose of perpetuating the two classes of society—the ruling class versus the working class. Gramsci said:

> If one wishes to break this pattern, one needs...to create a single type of formative school. [Antonio Gramsci, "On Education," p. 14]

Creating "a single type of formative school" is exactly what School-to-Work (STW) does. (See the author's *Fed Ed: The New Federal Curriculum and How It's Enforced* (St. Paul: EdWatch, 2002), Chapter 14.). School-to Work makes all education vocational. STW argues that no one should be educated beyond his station in life. Education becomes strictly utilitarian—existing for the supposed good of society as determined by the ruling elite but not existing for the good of the individual.

CONCLUSION

As is evident from the description of Antonio Gramsci above, the new federal education system is built on the ideological foundation of Gramsci. Much of what we call postmodernism would be more accurately called Gramsci-style Marxism. Postmodern math is also Marxist math of the Gramsci variety. Much of what is called "constructivism" is really the new Marxism. The educational term "radical constructivism" is really Marxism as defined by Gramsci. The federal education system's emphasis on discovery learning, group projects, authentic learning, and teachers as guides on the side, along with the formation of a unitary system of education, all follow Gramsci's recommendations for transformational education. We can call the new Federal Curriculum "postmodernist." We can call it "constructivist." If we wish to more exact, however, we should refer to it as "Marxism of the Gramsci variety," or simply, the "new Marxism."

What is the goal of transformational education? According to Gramsci, the goal is the total transformation of culture and society in order to create the world-wide Marxist state.

Why can the grade-school girl in Utah no longer succeed in math? The reason is that she is a pawn in a great global chess match over education now largely controlled by those who want to transform America at the expense of the children who simply want a good education. To the Marxists, individuals are not important. To the Marxists, every eye must be fixed on their utopian dream—and certainly not on an obsolete construct of the powerful called "mathematics."

CHAPTER FIVE

Multiculturalism

D avid Horowitz has explained that multiculturalism is really a political philosophy under the disguise of an academic philoso-phy. Multiculturalism, he says, is the political ideology of, once again, Italian Marxist, Antonio Gramsci. Multiculturalism, says Horowitz, is aggressively being taught in schools, especially in the language arts. Specifically, Horowitz said:

> The mentality [of multiculturalism] is Stalinist, but it is the particular Stalinism of Antonio Gramsci that forms the multicultural fervor of the academy. [David Horowitz, "Up From Multiculturalism," January, 1998, p. 1, *http://www.fiuedu/~yaf/multigarbage.html*]

Horowitz also said:

> What is multiculturalism? Well, in the first place, as my partner Peter Collier has pointed out, it is two lies in one word, since it is neither multi- nor cultural. It is, instead, fundamentally political and like Stalinism, allows only one party and one party line. Its bottom-line agenda is the deconstruction of the American nationality, in the service of the mindless, destructive, never-ending radical assault on the capital of the democratic world. Because it is the capital of the democratic world, multiculturalism is the banner of the hate-America Left. [*Ibid.* p. 2]

And:

> The question radicals faced at the time was: How to continue the war against the evil empire—America—now that socialism

was indisputably bankrupt? You do it the Gramsci way—
Antonio Gramsci being one of the many disreputable
Communists (and not a few disrespectable Nazis) who have
been enshrined as intellectual icons by the academic left.
Gramsci's addition to the Marxist theory was to suggest that by
seizing control of the culture you could extend that control to
the rest of the social order as well. [*Ibid.* p. 3]

And:

Along with this spiteful hatred, another socialist fission of the
multicultural movement is the post-modern view that everyone (except white people) and every culture (except Western
culture) is equal, and deserves equal respect. [*Ibid.* p. 3]

And:

It [multiculturalism] has simply moved on to another trench
in its permanent war against the West—the English and
Comp Lit departments in American Universities. [*Ibid.* p. 3]

The most prominent political scientist of our time, Samuel
Huntington, believes that the ideology of multiculturalism is now the
greatest threat to the freedom of the United States and to all of
Western civilization. Huntington said:

A more immediate and dangerous challenge exists in the
United States. Historically, American national identity has
been defined culturally by the heritage of Western civilization
and politically by the principles of the American Creed on
which Americans overwhelmingly agree: liberty, democracy,
individualism, equality before the law, constitutionalism, and
private property. In the late twentieth century both components of American identity have come under concentrated and
sustained onslaught from a small but influential number of
intellectuals and publicists. In the name of multiculturalism
they have attacked the identification of the United States
with Western civilization, denied the existence of common
American culture, and prompted racial, ethnic, and other
subnational cultural identities and groupings. They have
denounced, in the words of one of their reports, the "systematic bias toward European culture and its derivatives in

education..." In the 1990s the Clinton administration made the encouragement of diversity one of its major goals. [Samuel Huntington: *The Clash of Civilizations and the Remaking of World Order* (New York: Simon and Schuster, 1996), p. 305]

Huntington also said:

A multicultural United States will not be the United States; it will be the United Nations [world government]. [*Ibid.* p. 306]

As scholars Horowitz, Huntington and many others have said, multiculturalism is a political agenda masquerading as an educational agenda. As they have also said, multiculturalism is designed to undermine American freedom and sovereignty. Huntington has said that the future of the United States requires that it reject multiculturalism and reaffirm its national identity. [Ibid. p. 20] As Huntington and others have stated, multiculturalism is also dedicated to undermining Christianity.

Education, however, should include the academic study of other cultures. Education should also promote the principle of the equality of all people. How can we distinguish between the academic and legitimate study of other cultures, often called "cultural pluralism," versus the radical political and religious agenda known as multiculturalism?

The following rating system is intended to provide guidance in distinguishing between the legitimate academic study of cultures versus the advocacy of the radical political, religious and ecological multiculturalism worldview. The rating system can be used to evaluate textbooks, school objectives, state education standards and national education standards.

TWO KINDS OF MULTICULTURALISM

Cultural Pluralism

1. Emphasizes the principle that all people are equal but rejects the view that all cultures are equal.
2. Is academic, not political. Views the purpose of education as being the transmission of knowledge and academic skills. Rejects the view that education exists to transform society.
3. Insists on accurate and detailed information about different groups, both positive and negative.

4. Emphasizes the assimilation of various groups into a pluralistic American culture.
5. America is seen as a singular culture with many subcultures, a "melting pot." (Native Americans, as independent nations, are an exception to the rule.)
6. Recognizes that many of America's ideals have become more fully realized over time, when it has been possible to do so, but also believes that America is largely defined by its foundational principles.
7. Realizes that truth and morality are genuine, universal and real.
8. Recognizes both the positive and negative about the United States, but is also convinced that the United States is the leader of the free world.
9. Recognizes Western exceptionalism and American exceptionalism.
10. Realizes that no historical source is totally objective, but also believes that history is knowable, teachable and testable.

Radical Multiculturalism

1. Believes that all cultures are equal. It also intends that all groups have equal outcomes—on income, test scores, incarceration rates, use of natural resources, and the like.
2. Portrays government as being a creation of the powerful who use government to keep themselves in control and use government to exploit the weak and vulnerable.
3. Holds that the primary goal of education is changing attitudes, beliefs and behavior (transformational education) for the purpose of reconstructing all of society. The teaching of academic knowledge and skills is viewed as being secondary.
4. Regards education as being the training of social and political activists, as illustrated by service learning.
5. Is postmodernist and Marxist. Knowledge is viewed as being a tool by which the powerful subdue the vulnerable. Knowledge is not seen as truth. Even language and traditional academic disciplines such as mathematics are viewed as constructs. Knowledge is redefined to be a social construct arrived at by the consensus of those in power. Eliminating disparities between groups is seen as being more important than raising the achievement of all groups.
6. Because history is viewed as a construct by which the powerful subdue the vulnerable, history becomes the study of "multiple perspectives" on history and the study of the interaction of cultures.
7. Sees the goal of history classes as having students construct their own history. History is viewed as subjective. Knowledge is seen as being relative to the group and the individual.

8. Extends evolution to government and to other social institutions and constructs such as marriage, knowledge and culture. Evolution becomes a central explanatory paradigm for the social sciences as well as for the biological sciences.

9. Views morality, modesty, human rights and the family as being mere constructs. Believes that marriage is a creation of powerful males used to keep vulnerable females under subjection. Includes obscenity for the purpose of deconstructing student beliefs about modesty, morality and marriage.

10. Emphasizes the differences between groups, not assimilation of groups into a common American culture. Takes steps to maintain the differences—an example being bilingual education which is intended to retain cultural differences, not raise academic achievement.

11. Stresses America's failures or alleged failures as opposed to its successes. (Multiculturalism is anti-American.)

12. Undermines America's symbols and heroes. Thanksgiving, for example, is viewed as a day of mourning for Native Americans. Christopher Columbus is seen as a racist who supposedly committed acts of genocide. Portrays America as being a racist, sexist, and imperialist nation.

13. Minimizes or denies the importance of European culture in world history.

14. Ignores or minimizes the failures of any minority group.

15. Takes a negative view of individualism. Group identity and group rights are promoted instead. An emphasis on group projects and group grading is used to teach group identification and group consciousness.

16. Views capitalism as a method by which the powerful exploit the vulnerable.

17. Also sees private property rights as being exploitation of the vulnerable by the powerful.

18. Describes Christianity as a construct used by the powerful to exploit the masses. Rejects Christianity's claim to have "the truth." (Multiculturalism is opposed to Christianity and Judaism.)

19. Sees all cultures as being either part of the oppressor class or the oppressed class. (Multiculturalism is really biculturalism.)

20. Believes that since all cultures are equal, and since government needs to evolve, and since all countries need to be equal, and since America is merely trying to dominate the world and keep all other nations under its control, the time has come for all

nations to get together in a common world government where the United States will cease to be a free and independent nation and will instead be under the control of the United Nations.

Acceptance of homosexuality is included as part of "diversity" according to the Minnesota Department of Health's *School Health Guide*.

See also the writings of John Fonte (Hudson Institute), Richard Bernstein (New York literary critic), and the book *Where Did Social Studies Go Wrong?*, a report of the Thomas B. Fordham Foundation, August, 2003, [*http://www.edexcellence.net*].

Chapter Six

The New Pantheism

Pantheism has been around for a long time. It certainly is not new. Pantheism does, however, have a new outward form. Pantheism is the now the dominant form of New Age religion. The term "New Age" religion was coined by psychologist and pantheist, Carl Jung. According to Jung, religion evolves just as everything else evolves. For that reason, said Jung, religion is now reaching a higher level of realization than in the past. Science and religion, believed Jung, are today being integrated into one unified reality which is appropriate for our New Age.

Those familiar with modern psychology recognize that the theory of Carl Jung is very popular today. The influence of Jung is now greater that that of his early mentor, Sigmund Freud. Video catalogs on psychology, for example, will commonly list five or more videos on Jung for every video on Freud. The same disparity is true in comparing Jung to other giants in the field of psychology such as Carl Rogers, B. F. Skinner, Erik Erikson and Alfred Adler.

What is the new pantheism? The following statements will summarize its central doctrines:

1. Nature is God.

Earth is God. The universe is God. Creator and created are the same. Everything that exists is God. "Pan" means all, "theism" means God. Pantheism means everything is God. The Apostle Paul included pantheism in his description of pagan religions when he said:

> They exchanged the truth of God for a lie, and worshipped and served created things rather than the Creator—who is forever praised. Amen. [Romans 1:25]

Pantheism is the worship of all creation collectively instead of Creator. For that reason, pantheism is antithetical to Christianity, Judaism and Islam.

2. God is impersonal.

God is "the Force" of the *Star Wars* movie series. (*Star Wars* was widely recognized as based on New Age theology.) Since the natural world is impersonal, God, who is Nature, must be impersonal, too. God, therefore, is not a conscious being, nor a moral being, nor a rational being. God just is. Since God, who is Nature, has no rationality, truth and religion are mystical in essence.

3. Man is God.

Since pantheists see man as being part of Nature, and since Nature is seen as God, then man must be God, too. God also includes the animals, plants, rocks and all matter and all energy. Whatever exists is God. If man and animals are both God, then man and animals are brothers in a literal sense. Man and trees are brothers and sisters, also.

4. Man is not above Nature; man is one with nature.

Pantheists believe that Man was created by Nature. Man, therefore, is not the steward of Nature; Nature is the steward of man. If Nature is the steward of man, and since, for example, fires are natural and chain saws are not, it is better to let forests burn than to cut down any trees.

5. People are not individuals.

Pantheists say that what appears to be individualism is superficial and temporary. Death is casting off the appearance of individualism and personhood. Death is like a drop of water being absorbed back into the ocean of all existence. Identity is ultimately collective, not individualistic.

6. All things are one.

According to prominent New Age theologian Joseph Campbell, there is no dichotomy of good versus evil, God versus Satan, God versus Nature, man versus Nature, or church versus state. All things are one. Since there is no separation of church and state, the government should be promoting pantheism and doing so in a variety of ways, including by means of the education system. Since all things are one, being male or female is regarded as a matter of appearances only. Healthy personalities achieve a harmony in being both male and female. The Hindu symbol of the Mandela, representing the unity of all things, is embraced by the new pantheists. Paradise is defined as being in harmony with Nature, being one with Nature.

religions, the Earth religions, are correct.

lieve that the various pagan religions which in some
ature are true because they equate God with Nature.
are often called the mythology of indigenous peoples.
eligions include the occult, Wicca (witchcraft), astrology,
and relig.. that worship the sun, the rain, fertility, and the like. Also
included are religions of ancient Egyptians, early Germanic tribes, and
the paganism of early Scandinavians, Native Americans, and primitive
people from all over the globe.

8. Moral virtue is treating Nature as sacred.

If Nature is God, then anything natural is holy and must be treated
with corresponding respect. The great "sins" include cutting down trees,
especially in the rainforest, drilling for oil on the North Slope of Alaska,
repressing sexuality and engaging in any kind of pollution. Adultery,
pornography, abortion, euthanasia, and homosexuality are seen as being
morally good or morally neutral. Genetic experimentation and cloning of
human embryos are especially exciting to pantheists because they see
themselves as the creators of a new, advanced race of superhuman beings.

9. Evolution is true and defined broadly.

Pantheists see themselves as being scientific. They believe that cre-
ationism and evolution are both true. That is, they believe that evolution
is the method by which Nature, which is God, created the living world.
This doctrine partially explains the popularity of pantheism—its adherents can be evolutionists and creationists at the same time. Religion is
also seen as evolving; that is why the new pantheism is called New Age
Religion—it's the belief-system that is seen as fitting this New Age.
Evolution is defined so broadly that it includes the evolution of marriage,
knowledge, the Constitution of the United States and of all features of
government. Pantheists are emphatic in saying that their religion is scientific and that it harmonizes religion and science.

10. Man is the mind of Earth.

Pantheists compare the Universe to the human body—all existence
is seen as one interconnected unity but having different parts. Humans
are seen as being the "mind" of Earth and are regarded, therefore, as
being the instruments which will usher in the New Age of a higher
level of existence. The leaders of the pantheistic movement see themselves as being the new Masters who have been called to usher in this
utopian New Age. These "new Masters" say they are often in contact
with "Ascended Masters" who are seen as former Masters, now dead.

New Age leaders, such as Dr. Shirley McCune and Robert Muller, have said they are in contact with Ascended Masters of the spirit world.

11. The United Nations is the spiritual head of the new pantheistic world religion.

Robert Muller, former head of the education branch of UNESCO, is a well known New Age leader. Debra Rae described his view of the UN as follows:

> In *My Testament to the UN*, prize winning creator of the World Core Curriculum and occultist Robert Muller quotes a UN guru as having called the UN the "vision light of the Absolute Supreme." As former UN Assistant Secretary-General, Dr. Muller views the UN's spiritual dimension as inevitable. In fact, he dubs himself "Father of United Religions." [Debra Rae, *ABCs of Globalism: A Vigilant Christian's Glossary* (Lafayette, Louisiana: Huntington House Publishers, 1999), p. 303]

That is, the UN is seen as being the spiritual head of the worldwide New Age religion.

12. Christianity is the enemy.

Christianity, and to a lesser degree Islam, are seen as enemy religions by pantheists. Christianity claims to have exclusive and absolute truth, a position that pantheism rejects. Pantheists also object to Christianity's doctrine that God is outside of Nature and the creator of Nature. Christianity's views of sin, evil and the nature of man are also rejected by pantheists. New Age pantheists correctly recognize that Christianity is their primary obstacle to obtaining their one-world goals. Pantheists, along with humanists, argue the separation of church and state when it comes to issues such as displays of the Ten Commandments in the public square, but pantheists do not object to pantheism being promoted by the government and its schools. As noted above, promotion of pantheism by government schools is central to its plan for proselytizing.

13. Pantheistic evangelism is largely accomplished by reading myths.

Pantheists believe that people are drawn to their religion by the reading of pagan myths. Prominent New Age spokesman, Joseph Campbell, for example, when asked how pantheism should be spread, replied by saying:

Read myths. They teach you that you can turn inward, and you begin to get the message of the symbols. Read other people's myths, not those of your own religion, because you tend to interpret your own religion as facts—but if you read the other ones, you begin to get the message. [Joseph Campbell, *The Power of Myth* (New York: Anchor Books, 1991)]

This exhortation by Campbell, probably the most influential New Age theologian of our time, is extremely important because it explains how pantheists use our education system to win converts to their religion.

14. The world shall be one.

Since pantheists believe in the oneness of all things, it is not surprising that they look for the creation of a new, unified world. They intend to create a common world culture, a common pantheistic world religion, a world without national borders, and a world without nations that are separate, sovereign or independent. That is, they intend to create a world government, also called "world federalism." Since they recognize neither sin nor evil, they have no fear of centralizing all the governmental power of the world into one entity that will control the entire Earth. Since pantheists recognize no separation of church and state, it is natural that the one-world religion of pantheism and the one-world government of the UN would be one and the same.

This is the one overarching position that secular Humanism, pantheism, third-way economics of Anthony Giddens, postmodernism and the new Marxism all have in common—they all subscribe to the utopian dream of world government. It should not surprise us, then, to find that world government is the central unifying theme of the new Federal Curriculum since it is integral to all the worldviews contained within it. All these worldviews believe that world federalism is the next natural step in the evolution of government.

As noted above, the new pantheism also goes by the title "Gaia theology" or "Gaia hypothesis." "Gaia" is a Greek word meaning "earth." Our English word "geography" comes from the Greek "Gaia" with a soft "g" pronunciation and the Greek word "graphy" meaning "writing" as in "graphics." "Geography" literally means the "writing on the earth." NASA astrophysicist, James Lovelock, described Gaia as follows:

Gaia is Mother Earth. Gaia is immortal. She is the eternal source of life. She does not need to reproduce herself as she is immortal. She is certainly the mother of us all, including Jesus. [Ross Evans West, "Gaia—She's Alive: A Conversation with James Lovelock," *Orion Nature Quarterly* 8:1, 1989, p. 58]

Pantheism/New Age religion has a large following in the United States. The author recently estimated the number of different New Age books on the shelves at a local Barnes and Noble Booksellers store and concluded that over 1,000 different New Age titles were available on the shelves. Someone is buying and reading these books.

The pantheists are having a huge impact on the culture of the United States. Chuck Colson and Nancy Pearcy described their presence as follows:

> *American Demographics* magazine, summarizing a demographic study done in 1997, noted that there has been a "comprehensive shift in values, worldviews, and ways of life"…[of many Americans. They are the] "Cultural Creatives." They embrace a new "trans-modernist" set of values, including "environmentalism, feminism, global issues, and spiritual searching." They often have a background in movements for social justice, civil rights, feminism, and New Age spirituality. Thoroughly postmodernist, they are skeptical, if not resentful, of moral absolutes. They "see nature as sacred," and emphasize self-actualization and spiritual growth. [Charles Colson and Nancy Pearcey, *How Now Shall We Live?* (Wheaton: Tyndale House Publishers, Inc., 1999), p. 25]

Colson and Pearcy have accurately captured the belief-system of many of those who wish to transform America into something totally different from what it is today. Not all of them are pantheists, of course. The world federalists operate as a coalition. Some members of this coalition have worldviews that are remarkably similar to each other. Other groups have views which appear to be diametrically opposed to one another. They work together because they share some goals in common. They operate just as all political coalitions operate.

As noted above, most members of this coalition have one core belief in common—they want to replace American independence and sovereignty with the utopian dream of world government. To achieve this goal, the new millennialists recognize that they must change the American culture. How does one change an entire culture? The revolutionaries recognize that changing a culture requires changing its religion. That is why a focal point of the education agenda of the revolutionaries is inculcating pantheism/New Age religion into the hearts and minds of our youth.

Chapter Seven

Pantheism in High Places

One of the most influential people at the United Nations is Maurice Strong. Strong, for example, was Secretary General of the 1992 Earth Summit, an event which largely defined the nature of world-wide environmentalism.

Maurice and his wife, Hanne, own and operate a 63,000 acre ranch in Colorado called Baca Grande. This ranch is a world center for worship and other gatherings of New Age, pagan, pantheistic and Eastern religions. Hanne Strong, a New Age priestess, has spoken in over 90 countries on what she calls, "spiritually based environmental education."

By means of his position at UNESCO, Strong promotes Gaia worship. Strong is also the director of the Temple of Understanding in New York, one for four centers of pantheism/New Age worship in the United States. He uses the Temple to encourage Americans concerned about the environment to replace Christianity with the worship of Mother Earth.

In his opening address to the Earth Summit, conference Secretary-General Strong said:

> It is the responsibility of every human being today to choose between the force of darkness and the force of light. We must, therefore, transform our attitudes and values and adopt a renewed respect for the superior laws of Divine Nature.

All of the United Nations' treaties, declarations, protocols and other documents dealing with either education or the environment are based on pantheism as promoted by Maurice Strong.

The UN's Biodiversity Assessment, for example, which is part of the Biodiversity Treaty, states:

> The western world is...characterized by the denial of the sacred attributes of nature...[which] became firmly established about 2000 years ago with the Judeo-Christian-Islamic religious traditions ...The world views of traditional societies tend to be strikingly different.... They view themselves as members of a community that includes other humans, but also rocks, springs and pools. People are then members of a community of beings—living and non-living. Thus rivers are viewed as mothers. Animals may be treated as kin...

That is, the Biodiversity Treaty in effect says that the monotheistic religions of Christianity, Judaism and Islam are destructive to environmental concerns because these religions treat God and nature as being separate. The religions of indigenous peoples, in contrast, are pictured as being environmentally friendly because they believe that God and Nature are one and the same.

The U. S. Senate came within 24 hours of ratifying the radical Biodiversity Treaty. The Senate was prevented from doing so by Dr. Michael Coffman and several others who, less than 48 hours before the scheduled vote, brought documentation to the Senate which demonstrated what the treaty actually meant. As a consequence of this information, the treaty was never voted on by the U.S. Senate. For a detailed description of the pantheistic nature of various UN treaties and actions, see Michael Coffman. [*Saviors of the Earth?* (Chicago: Northfield Publishing) 1994].

The Earth Charter was one of the documents presented to the 1992 Earth Summit. The Earth Charter (see Appendix C) is a pantheistic document. The Earth Charter:

- Uses the word "sacred" once.
- Uses the word "reverence" twice.
- Uses the word "spiritual" seven times, including the term "spiritual education" (used once).
- Always capitalizes "Earth" and always uses it without the article "the."
- Is housed in the "Arc of Hope" modeled after the Arc of the Covenant.

The World Pantheist Movement website lists the Earth Charter as one of the fundamental documents which define the World Pantheist Movement. [http://www.pantheism.net] The Earth Charter is called a "charter" and is contained in the "Arc of Hope" because it is seen as being a covenant between man and Nature.

The Earth Charter summarizes the views of environmentalism and sustainable development followed by the United Nations. It is also the consensus statement of faith of the major environmental organizations world-wide. These organizations include the Sierra Club, Green Cross International, Earth First!, Friends of the Earth and many others. The Earth Charter is to the UN and the international environmental groups what the Apostle's Creed is to Christians. It would be difficult to overstate its significance.

What is "sustainable development"?

The Earth Charter clarifies that all international agreements dealing with the environment are created for the purpose of establishing "sustainable development." What does "sustainable development" mean in these international agreements? These are the positions the Earth Charter includes under the term "sustainable development":

1. Earth worship (pantheism).
2. Evolution, broadly defined.
3. Socialized medicine.
4. World federalism.
5. Animal rights (animals are seen as our brothers and sisters).
6. Income redistribution among nations and within nations.
7. Eradication of genetically modified (GMO) crops.
8. Contraception and "reproductive health" (legal abortion).
9. World-wide "education for sustainability" which includes spiritual education.
10. Debt forgiveness for third-world nations.
11. Adoption of the gay rights agenda.
12. Elimination of nuclear weapons and the right to bear arms.
13. Redefining the media so it will support the environmental agenda, not report on it.
14. Setting aside biosphere reserves where no human presence is allowed.

As is obvious from the 14 points above, "sustainable development" as defined by the Earth Charter includes a broad religious, ideological and political agenda. The focal point is religious, however. All the other belief statements follow from the Charter's core belief of pantheism.

How does the Earth Charter hope to accomplish its agenda as defined by the Charter? The Earth Charter webpage answers that question by saying:

Education is the key to advancing the transition to more sustainable ways of living. Transformative education is needed: ...The Earth Charter provides a unique framework for developing educational programs and curricula aimed at transformative learning for a more just, sustainable and peaceful world.

Notice again what this language says. The Earth Charter web page did not merely say that education is "a key" to sustainable development as the Charter defines it. The Earth Charter said education is "the key" to sustainable development. The United Nations and the worldwide environmental organizations intend to accomplish their radical goals by establishing "education for sustainability," as they define the term, in all the nations of the world including the United States.

That was in 1992. Has the agenda of the UN changed since that time? Not at all. In July of 2003, UNESCO, the education arm of the UN, announced its plans to declare the years 2005 to 2014 to be the "Decade of Education for Sustainable Development." (UNESCO stands for United Nations Education, Scientific and Cultural Organization.) In its draft of what UNESCO called its "International Implementation Scheme," UNESCO said:

Thus, education is the primary agent of transformation toward sustainable development...The international community now strongly believes that we need to foster—through education—the values, behavior and lifestyles required for a sustainable future. [p. 4 of the Draft Statement]

Notice that UNESCO said "education is the primary agent of transformation toward sustainable development" and that transformational education for sustainability focuses on changing the "values, behavior and lifestyles" of the student. One wonders how UNESCO could have made itself more clear.

Does this "transformational education for sustainability" include the United States? The year was 1990. The international agreement was called the "World Declaration on Education for All." George Bush, Sr., President of the United States, signed the agreement on behalf of the United States. In the action plan of the agreement, known as the "Framework for Action," the United States agreed to the following "targets for the 1990s":

(6) Increased acquisition by individuals and families of the knowledge, skills and values required for better living and

sustainable development...with effectiveness assessed in terms of behavioral change. [pp. 4&5]

By signing the World Declaration on Education for All, President George Bush, Sr. committed the United States to teaching sustainable development. Since this World Declaration on Education for All (EFA) is an international agreement much like the Earth Charter, there is no reason to define "sustainable development" differently than it is defined by the Earth Charter or differently than it is defined in all the international agreements, for that matter. The definition is the same in all the agreements.

Now fast-forward ten years to April 28, 2000. The United States President at this time is Bill Clinton. President Clinton, on behalf of the United States, signed the updated version of the World Declaration on Education for All known as the "Dakar Framework for Action" at the World Education Forum. President Clinton, at this forum, agreed to an action plan that said:

Education was defined as a fundamental human right and the key to sustainable development and peace. [p.1]

Notice the repetition in the critical language of these agreements: "Education was defined as...**the key** to sustainable development." And "...education is **the primary agent** of transformation toward sustainable development." And "Education is **the key** to advancing the transition to more sustainable ways of living" (emphasis added).

Those who have overseen and drafted the international agreements have a crystal-clear purpose—they intend to use the education systems of the countries of the world to aggressively advance their agenda of sustainable development. By "sustainable development" they mean a broad religious, ideological and political agenda that centers on pantheism. Keep in mind that pantheists recognize no separation of church and state. Using government and government schools to promote pantheism is an integral part of their plan. This is the plan that the United States has now agreed several times to carry out.

We shouldn't be too surprised, therefore, if we find that our education system is doing exactly what our Presidents have agreed it will do.

CHAPTER EIGHT

Teaching Pantheism in the Schools

New Age religion is now aggressively being taught in our nation's public schools. A Minnesota charter school, for example, has developed an environmental curriculum that is being promoted and used throughout the United States. The U.S. Department of Education has labeled this school a "model school." The curriculum requires the following activities and resources:

- Discussion of aesthetic/spiritual values of water in *Walden*
- View the *Spirit of Nature* video (Dalai Lama & Native American elder)
- *Encounters with the Archdruid* discussions
- *Nile: River of the Gods* video
- *Spirit in Nature* film clip with Dalai Lama
- "A Tibetan Buddhist Perspective on Spirit in Nature"
- "Mother Earth: Nature as Living System"
- *Hero with a Thousand Faces* by Joseph Campbell

This model curriculum is clearly centered on pantheism. Joseph Campbell, whose books are required reading in the curriculum, is one of the leading pantheistic theologians of our time. (Much of what passes for environmental education and multiculturalism is really indoctrination in pantheistic/New Age theology.) The ACLU and similar organizations have no objections to public schools indoctrinating our children with pantheistic beliefs. It is only Christianity that these organizations object to.

Pantheism is included in every area of the federal education system. The federal government's own achievement test, the NAEP, for example, includes the following reading selection (in the eighth grade language arts test):

...there once was a Lakota holy man called Drinks Water who dreamed what was to be, and this was before the coming of the [whites]. He dreamed that the four-leggeds were going back into the earth and that a strange race had woven a spider's web around the Lakotas. And he said: "When this happens, you shall live in square gray houses, in a barren land, and beside those gray houses you shall starve." They say he went back to Mother Earth soon after he saw this vision, and it was sorrow that killed him.

This reading selection promotes pantheism. After reading this selection, the student is required to answer a series of questions about the reading. Students who are schooled in pantheism have an obvious advantage in answering the questions. (The actual questions are not quoted here because No Child Left Behind made it a felony to disclose a single NAEP question. The federal change-agents do not want the public to know what is on this radical test.)

Pantheism is being taught in every area of the Federal Curriculum. The primary method by which it is being promoted, however, is through the language arts curriculum. The National Council for the Social Studies (NCSS), for example, has published a canon of recommended children's literature which includes a substantial dose of pantheism. This NCSS canon is the subject of its book, *Children's Literature in Social Studies: Teaching to the Standards*. The book clarifies its position as it says:

A fresh era of thought about teaching the social studies began in 1994 when National Council for the Social Studies (NCSS)...described the social studies as "the integrated study of social sciences to promote civic competence." [p. 9]

Children's Literature in Social Studies: Teaching to the Standards, also says:

Visions of effective social studies learning experiences include literature-based instruction in which children's books are used as a basis for teaching social studies. [p. 9.]

As can be seen from these statements, a new approach to teaching social studies emerged in 1994. This is the year that Goals 2000, School-to-Work and HR6 were signed into law by then President Bill Clinton. These are the bills which authorized the U.S Department of Education to establish curriculum standards for all schools. The purpose of the NCSS book mentioned above is to demonstrate to schools how they can comply with the national social studies curriculum standards by means of their language arts program. The book even has a table which explains which theme of the Federal Curriculum is contained in each recommended book.

The oldest copyright date for any of the selections in the canon is 1990—meaning that all the classics have been omitted. The primary criteria for choosing this literature was not literary merit, obviously. Nor was the primary criteria that of usefulness in teaching language arts. The primary reason these selections are in the recommended canon is because they teach the Federal Curriculum, including pantheism.

The following examples from the NCSS canon will reveal how pantheism is being promoted in this book. (The titles of the books, along with portions of the annotations included with the books, will explain the content of the works.)

One of the recommended books in *Children's Literature in Social Studies: Teaching to the Standards*, along with a brief NCSS description, is the following:

> *AANI AND THE TREE HUGGERS.* This fictionalized picture story…recounts the origins of the Chipko Andolan (Hug the Tree) Movement in northern India in the 1970's. When men from the city came into rural areas to cut down trees, women villagers successfully stopped them by embracing individual trees….

Why did the women wrap themselves around the trees? Because the trees were viewed as being their brothers and sisters. Cutting down trees is pictured as being similar to cutting up living human beings. Another selection in the recommended canon is the following:

> *CUTTERS, CARVERS AND THE CATHEDRAL,* Daily visitors to the Cathedral of St. John the Divine in New York City see a working cathedral where worship, festivals, concerts, art exhibits and lectures are held….

This selection is especially significant. Of all the cathedrals in the United States, why does NCSS recommend a story giving us a guided tour, including pictures, of this one? The reason is that the Cathedral of St. John the Divine is one of four pantheism/New Age religion centers in the United States. The other three are in Colorado, San Francisco, and one more in New York. What are chances that the NCSS canon just happened to include a pantheistic center by chance? New Age guru, Deepak Chopra, says, "There are no coincidences." [*Star Tribune*, April 4, 2004] The inclusion of literature on the Cathedral of St. John the Divine in the NCSS canon makes it obvious that pantheism is deliberately being promoted by the canon.

Another selection in the canon reads as follows:

> *THE INDIAN WAY: LEARNING TO COMMUNICATE WITH MOTHER EARTH,*...each of Grandpa Iron's stories teaches reverence for nature and respect for Mother Earth. The book includes suggestions for creative activities that children can undertake to help them remember the ecological lesson inherent in each of the thirteen stories.

"Learning to communicate with Mother Earth" is pantheism. Another NCSS selection is the following:

> *GIVING THANKS: A NATIVE AMERICAN GOOD MORNING MESSAGE,*...the text of this picture book carries the 'ancient message of peace and appreciation for Mother Earth and all her inhabitants' to her family.... Children of these native peoples are taught the concept of greeting the world each morning by saying thank you to all living things, which is what this picture-book expresses

Why would we say "thank you" to "Mother Earth"? We would do so only if Earth is God. This book, by the way, is recommended for pre-school children. How well-equipped are three to five year-olds to critically evaluate what they read? This is indoctrination of our most vulnerable citizens. Another children's book recommended by NCSS is the following:

> *MUSICIANS OF THE SUN,* "Out of the starry night he came, invisible, untouchable, Lord of the Night. King of the Gods. Soul of the World." Dramatic language introduces the principal Aztec deity whose name means "Smoking Mirror."

Remember that New Age theologian Joseph Campbell said the way to win converts to pantheism/New Age religion is to have people read the myths of other cultures. That is why the above selection is included. Another NCSS recommended book is:

MY TWO UNCLES, Elly loves her two uncles—her father's brother Ned and his partner Phil.... An unusually realistic account of a young child's struggle to understand the complexities of homophobia within her extended family...

The selection above is one of several children's books in the canon which promotes the homosexual agenda. Neither pantheistic morality, nor the National Council for the Social Studies, finds any fault with homosexual activities. Still another NCSS selection is the following:

THE LITTLE LAMA OF TIBET, A child is recognized as the incarnation of Ling Rinpoche, the late tutor of the Dalai Lama. He lives in exile in the mountains of Dhramsala, India, studying scriptures, reading religious stories, and otherwise preparing to pass on Buddhist teachings to his people. This monk was six years old in the year Raimondo was granted permission to photograph him. Her photographs are reproduced in full color...

This is a children's story of a six-year-old child who is described as being the reincarnation of a former holy man. Notice that the selection does not say that the boy "claims" to be this reincarnation. According to the NCSS description, the boy actually is the reincarnation. The story includes color photographs of this kid who is being passed off as the reincarnation of the tutor of the Dalai Lama.

Approximately eight percent of the recommended readings in the NCSS canon advocate pantheism along the lines described above. This proselytizing operates under the cover of multiculturalism and environmentalism, but it is really pantheism, pure and simple.

The recommended ages for these books are for children between 3 and 12 years of age. Most of them are written for children in the first through fifth grades. How many first through fifth graders are able to critically evaluate what they read? How about the three-year olds on the low end; can they critically evaluate what they are hearing? They have the story read to them. They are shown the pictures. Do they see these stories as being a part of the real world? Absolutely. The change-agents know what they are doing. They are indoctrinating our youngest and most vulnerable citizens with pantheism, and most of the time the parents have no idea what is happening.

Should we be surprised? In several international agreements signed by the Presidents of the United States, we agreed to teach sustainable development. As we have seen, the international definition of "sustainable development" is centered on pantheism. Why should we be surprised to find our nation doing what it several times has agreed to do?

Pantheism is diametrically opposed to the description of Genesis, chapter one, which says: "In the beginning God created the heavens and the earth." Pantheism is similarly opposed to any claim of truth apart from its own theology. Such a truth-claim is stated in the Gospel of John, chapter one, which reads:

> In the beginning was the Word, and the Word was with God, and the Word was God. He was with God in the beginning. Through him all things were made; without him nothing was made that has been made. In him was life, and that life was the light of men. The light shines in the darkness, but the darkness has not understood it.... [verses 1-6] [and]

> For God so loved the world that he gave his one and only Son, that whoever believes in him shall not perish but have eternal life. For God did not send his Son into the world to condemn the world, but to save the world through him. [verses 16-17]

As David Horowitz has said, literature classes are now the preferred area for teaching the broad and radical political agenda known as multiculturalism. [David Horowitz, "Up From Multiculturalism," January, 1998, p. 1. http://www.fiuedu/~yaf/multigarbage.html] (See Appendix B.) Every selection in this NCSS canon of literature promotes either multiculturalism or pantheism. According the National Council of Social Studies, and according to the new Federal Curriculum, language arts now exists for the purpose of transforming the worldview of the child to conform to the agenda of multiculturalism and pantheism/New Age religion. (See also Chapter 21.)

CHAPTER NINE

International Agreements

The most significant international agreement regarding education policy is the "World Declaration on Education for All." This agreement was formulated in 1990. The agreement was the result of a summit sponsored by the United Nations called "The World Conference on Education for All." Then President George Bush, Sr. signed the Declaration on behalf of the United States.

A UN "declaration," once signed by the United States President, is an example of "soft law." "Declarations," "protocols," "agreements" and the like have largely replaced treaties on the international stage. They do not have the standing of treaties in the United States unless they are submitted to the U.S. Senate and ratified by a 2/3 vote. They are, nonetheless, statements of policy of the United States if signed by the executive branch of government. Since the Department of Education, along with all other federal departments, is administered by the executive branch of government, these signed agreements have the effect of law and have, therefore, enormous influence on government policy.

The World Declaration on Education for All (EFA) consists of two parts: The first part contains the structure of the agreement; the second part consists of the action plan or policy agreement. The EFA policy agreement, which is the most important part, is called the "Framework for Action." It says:

> This **Framework for Action**...derives from the **World Declaration on Education for All** [and] is intended as a guide for national governments...in formulating their own plans of action for implementing the **World Declaration on Education for All** ...by the year 2000.

When President Bush signed this international agreement, he committed the United States to implementing its plan of action. For that reason we should expect the federal government's education policies, especially the Goals 2000 law, to implement EFA. Even the title of the bill—Goals 2000—is right out of the international agreement. That is, EFA consisted of education goals the United States agreed to complete by the year 2000.

How do we know that Goals 2000 was actually based on this international agreement? The following comparison of the eight national goals of Goals 2000 to the goals the United States agreed to in the World Declaration on Education for All will answer that question. Goals 2000 goes somewhat further than EFA—a feature that EFA encourages all countries to enact. The critical point is that all of the stipulations of EFA are included in the Goals 2000 law—as can be seen from the following eight goals and their comparison to EFA:

Goal 1 of Goals 2000 reads:

GOAL 1: Ready to Learn: By the year 2000, all children will start school ready to learn.

The United States Department of Education constructed a series of "indices" which were the criteria used to measure how well the eight goals of Goals 2000 were being met. The first index for measuring Goal One was expansion of early childhood education. In the World Declaration on Education for All, the United States agreed to:

Address the basic learning needs of all means: early childhood care and development opportunities…. Targets [include]… expansion of early childhood care and development activities [by the year 2000].

As we can see, therefore, Goal 1 of Goals 2000, as defined by the index of early childhood education expansion, fulfills the early childhood portion of the EFA agreement. The second goal of Goals 2000 reads:

GOAL 2: School Completion: By the year 2000, the high school graduation rate will increase to at least 90 percent.

In the World Declaration on Education for All, the United States agreed that:

Targets [include]…improvement in learning achievement such that an agreed percentage…attains or surpasses a defined level of necessary learning achievement…. by the year 2000.

By defining "necessary learning achievement" as high school graduation, Goal 2 completes another stipulation of EFA. The third goal of Goals 2000 reads:

GOAL 3: Student achievement and citizenship: By the year 2000, all students will leave grades 4, 8, and 12 having demonstrated competency over challenging subject matter including English, mathematics, science, foreign languages, civics and government, economics, arts, history, geography and every school in America will ensure that all students learn to use their minds well, so they may be prepared for responsible citizenship, further learning, and productive employment in our nation's modern economy.

In the World Declaration on Education for All, the United Stated agreed to:

[Achieve] universal access to, and completion of …whatever higher level of education is considered "basic" by the year 2000. [And that] the basic learning needs be met, including cognitive skills, values, attitudes, as well as subject knowledge.

As part of Goal 3, all states were required to adopt basic competency tests which would meet this portion of EFA. The Federal Curriculum, put in place as part of Goals 2000, stipulates that student achievement consists of attitudes and values along with cognitive skills. Once again Goals 2000 was structured to meet the stipulations of the international agreement. The fourth goal states:

GOAL 4: Teacher Education and Professional Development: By the year 2000, the Nation's teaching force will have access to programs for the continued improvement of their professional skills and the opportunity to acquire the knowledge and skills needed to instruct and prepare students for the next century.

In the World Declaration on Education for All, the United States Agreed to:

[By the year 2000] depending on the outcomes desired, teachers have to be trained accordingly, whilst benefiting from in-service programmes as well as other incentives of opportunity which put a premium on the achievement of these outcomes. [And] pre and in-service training programmes for key personnel should be initiated or strengthened where they do exist.

Our teacher continuing education programs include pre-service and in-service programs, just like EFA requires. Goal five of Goals 2000 reads:

GOAL 5: Mathematics and Science: By the year 2000, United States students will be first in the world in mathematics and science achievement.

Goal five of Goals 2000 is the only U.S. goal not contained in the World Declaration on Education for All. As observed above, countries can add to what they agreed to in the World Declaration, but they cannot subtract from the agreement. Other nations would obviously not agree that the United States should be first in the world in student achievement in math and science. As we have seen, however, integrated math, which is part of the Goals 2000 program in the United States, has actually reduced the math and science achievement of our students. Because the achievement tests are now based on integrated math, however, we no longer have a valid measure for comparing the math achievement of U.S. students to other students of the world. The fifth goal was included in Goals 2000 for public relations purposes only. It obviously has not been met.

Goal 5 can, however, also be viewed as meeting the following language in the World Declaration on Education for All:

Time-bound targets convey a sense of urgency. [And] Specify expected attainments and outcomes...within an appropriate time-frame. [And targets include] expansion of...essential skills required of youth.

The sixth goal of Goals 2000 reads:

GOAL 6: Adult literacy and lifelong learning: By the year 2000, every adult American will be literate and will possess the knowledge and skills necessary to compete in a global economy and exercise the rights and responsibility of citizenship.

In the World Declaration on Education for All, the United States agreed to a:

Reduction of the adult illiteracy rate...by the year 2000.

Once again the "National Goal" of Goals 2000 includes the goals the United States agreed to in the World Declaration on Education for All. The seventh goal reads:

GOAL 7: Safe, Disciplined and Alcohol and Drug-Free Schools: By the year 2000, every school in the United States will be free of drugs, violence, and the unauthorized presence of firearms and alcohol and will offer a disciplined environment conducive to learning.

Goals 2000 was adopted before school shootings became common in the United States—certainly raising questions about the degree to which we have achieved goal seven. In the World Declaration on Education for All, the United States agreed that:

By the year 2000...[nations will prioritize] rehabilitating dilap-idated schools. [while]... upgrading building and facilities... [while] preventing drug abuse.

Once again Goals 2000 goes beyond EFA but also meet the EFA requirement. The eighth goal of Goals 2000 reads:

GOAL 8: Parental participation: By the year 2000, every school will promote partnerships that will increase parental involvement and participation in promoting the social, emo-tional and academic growth of children.

In the World Declaration on Education for All, the United States agreed that:

Many partners must join with education authorities...This implies the active involvement of a wide range of partners—families, teachers.... Family resources, including time and mutual support are vital for the success of basic education activities [and should be enlisted by the year 2000].

The Goals 2000 contracts the states signed with the federal gov-ernment includes the broad range of partners stipulated by EFA—

"partners" included parents, businesses, local governments and other educational institutions.

There are a total of eight national goals that were part of the Goal 2000 law. As can be seen from the quotations and other information above, there is a remarkable similarity between these eight goals and the goals of the Action Plan for the World Declaration on Education for All (EFA). This similarity could be accidental, of course, but the similarities do not end there. In the international agreement the United States also said it would abide by the following requirements:

1. EFA requires nations to: "Specify...indicators and procedures to be used to monitor progress in reaching the targets." Goals 2000 required all states to submit a yearly report consisting of "indices" which measure the state's progress in meeting the eight national goals. The state reports describing progress on these indices are matters of public record and should be available at every state's department of education.

2. EFA requires nations to: "Specify...an implementation strategy and timetable." The Goals 2000 law primarily consists of an implementation strategy and timetable.

3. EFA requires nations to: "[Allow] international partners [to] assist countries, through direct support and through regional cooperation, to complete this preparatory stage. 1990-1992)...Development agencies [UNESCO shall] establish policies for monitoring progress at regional and international levels (1990-1993)" In EFA the United States agreed to have UNESCO (a branch of the UN) assist and monitor its progress on EFA goals. Every year the United States reports to UNESCO on the progress it is making toward the goals it agreed to in the World Declaration on Education for All. The United States completed the planning phase of this agreement in 1993 and adopted the implementation plan (Goals 2000 and School-to-Work) in 1994, right on schedule.

4. EFA requires that: "Governments...undertake comprehensive policy reviews." The United States compiles yearly policy reviews. They are available at state departments of education and state libraries. These reviews are called the yearly *Report of the National Goals Panel*. UNESCO also makes periodic policy reviews.

5. EFA requires that: "Governments, organizations and development agencies evaluate achievements and undertake comprehensive policy review at regional and global levels in (2000-2001)."

The policy review and update by the United Nations occurred on April 26-28, 2000, at what was called the "World Education Forum." The international agreement that resulted is called, "The Dakar Framework for Action." This "Framework for Action" is an updated action-plan of Education for All. President Bill Clinton signed the agreement on behalf of the United States. In order to comply with this new, updated education agreement, the United States, in January of 2002, adopted a new federal education law known as "No Child Left Behind."

Since the United States agreed to the Action Plan for the UN's World Declaration on Education for All, 1990, should we be surprised that the federal government's education programs—especially Goals 2000—were designed to fulfill that UN agreement? The only surprise would be if the federal government's initiatives did **not** satisfy the international agreement. As noted above, even the title of the American Bill—"Goals 2000"—is right out of the Education for All agreement, which stipulated that countries formulate their education policies based on goals to be accomplished by the year 2000.

Americans will be surprised to learn about the international connections to our education system, the reason being that the media has never informed the public about it. Why is this? It might be because many of the international agreements of recent years require the media to support the agreements. Such agreements include EFA, Agenda 21, and the UN Treaty on Biodiversity. The media has become a partner in the international agenda, and the media recognizes that many United States citizens would be outraged if they knew about the international connections to our education laws.

The same is true for most members of Congress. Many federal lawmakers would refuse to support the federal education programs if they knew about the international connections to those programs. For that reason, most federal lawmakers, like the public, have been kept in the dark about the international education agenda.

CHAPTER TEN

No Child Left Behind

O n October 3, 2003, U.S. Secretary of Education, Rod Paige, presented a speech to UNESCO. (UNESCO stands for United Nations Educational, Scientific and Cultural Organization.) In that speech Secretary Paige said:

> UNESCO, through the great leadership of Director General Matsuura, knows the importance of education on a global level by coordinating the *Education For All* initiative. *Education for All* is consistent with our recent education legislation, the *No Child Left Behind Act....* UNESCO is a powerful forum for sharing our views, developing a common strategy, and implementing joint action. [http://www.ed.gov/news/speeches/2003/10/10032003. html]

In other words according to Paige, America's education policy is part of an international effort coordinated by the UN which includes a "common strategy" and "joint action" among the international community, including the United States. Paige made these remarks in 2003, three years after President Clinton signed the updated action plan for EFA. For that reason, Paige's statement that NCLB is consistent with EFA also means that America's education policy is consistent with the 2000 update of EFA.

The updated version of EFA is the "The Dakar Framework for Action." This Framework for Action is the policy agreement which came out of the World Education Forum, sponsored by the United Nations, held on April 26-28, 2000, at Dakar, Senegal.

This action plan was signed by 187 countries of the world. President Bill Clinton signed the policy statement on behalf of the

United States. The key features of this action plan, as they have been implemented by NCLB, are as follows:

1. The Dakar Framework requires that nations expand early childhood education. No Child Left Behind includes a large number of federal grants to states for expanding early childhood education. This policy is an important part of NCLB even though a large number of studies have demonstrated that early childhood education provides no benefit for student achievement past the third grade.
2. The Dakar Framework requires nations to measure learning outcomes for all students in mathematics and reading. NCLB requires all states to test students each year in grades 3-8 and once in grades 9-12 in mathematics and reading.
3. The Dakar Framework requires that nations raise all students to proficiency levels in reading and mathematics by no later than 2015. NCLB requires states to raise all students to proficiency levels in reading and math by 2014.
4. The Dakar Framework requires that nations adopt "national action plans" for complying with the Dakar objectives by no later than 2002. NCLB, which is the national action plan in compliance with Dakar, was signed into law in 2002.
5. The Dakar Framework explains that it is a "reaffirmation of the vision" outlined in the World Declaration on Education for All. Michael Cohen, Assistant Secretary of Education under Bill Clinton, said that NCLB "builds squarely on the foundation laid down in Goals 2000." [Michael Cohen, paper delivered to the Thomas B. Fordham Foundation, February 12, 2002]
6. The Dakar Framework requires countries to eliminate the learning gaps based on ethnicity, race and economic circumstances no later than 2015. NCLB requires all states to eliminate the learning gaps based on ethnicity, race and economic circumstances by 2014. NCLB further requires states to report student scores based on gender, ethnicity, race and economic status.
7. The Dakar Framework requires nations to increase national funding for education. The "News in Brief" publication of UNESCO, in reporting on the Dakar Forum, stated that:

Gene Sperling, economic advisor to the President of the United States, announced at the Forum today that his government will increase by 50% its funding of education this year. He further said that the US administration will expand debt relief to countries that make a commitment to basic education [another stipulation of Dakar].

UNESCO clearly saw this statement by Sperling as a promise being made by the United States regarding its compliance with the Dakar Framework. No Child Left Behind, enacted in 2002, is part of an overall 48% increase in federal K-12 education spending. [*National* Review, March 8, 2004, p. 37] President George W. Bush specifically used the 50% education spending increase as a campaign issue in his 2004 re-election bid. The point is this—Gene Sperling presented the funding increase in NCLB as being partial fulfillment of the commitment of the United States to implement the international agreement made at Dakar. Not surprising, the actual funding increase matched his promise.

8. The Dakar Framework requires nations to make a "regular assessment of progress" in meeting the Dakar goals. As mentioned above, NCLB meets this stipulation by requiring all states to test all students each year in reading and math in grades 3-8 and once in grades 9-12.
9. The Dakar Framework requires "enhanced data collection" on students. NCLB includes so many stipulations for data collection that it is often referred to as the "federal government's data collection act."
10. The Dakar Framework stipulates that UNESCO will continue as the Secretariat for the enforcement of EFA and the Dakar Framework. The United State continues to send yearly reports to UNESCO on its progress on meeting the requirements of EFA and the Dakar Framework.

As is obvious from the ten points above, No Child Left Behind is the fulfillment of the Dakar Agreement of 2000. All the central features of NCLB are contained in this international accord. Once again, no one bothered to tell the Congress, nor the people of the United States, that this international agreement is the driving force behind our nation's federal education laws.

We now return to the grade-school girl in Utah who can no longer succeed in math because her school had switched to integrated math. Why is this happening to this grade-school girl as well as to millions of other grade-school children? What about the millions of elementary-school boys and girls throughout our nation who are being indoctrinated in multiculturalism and pantheism/New Age Religion? Why is this happening? Why is this, and much more, the order of the day for children all over the United States of America? The answers to these questions are at Dakar. Our children have become pawns of an inner circle of power at the international level. The rest of this book will further explain how it works.

CHAPTER ELEVEN

Taking Over the Schools

How did the federal government's Department of Education succeed in taking over education policy for all 50 states? After all, the United States Constitution makes it clear that education matters are reserved for the states and local units of government. How did the federal government succeed in taking over the schools?

A significant insight into that question is contained in the progress report submitted by the federal government to UNESCO in the year 2000. That progress report said:

> Most countries have national curricula and even national examinations,...In the United States, however, education is managed at the state and local levels...Thus, the very concept of designing and agreeing on a [national] set of learning outcomes across traditional jurisdictional lines is new, and in the minds of many, unsettling and undesirable. [p. 12 of the progress report]

In other words, the federal Department of Education could not directly set up a national curriculum because there would be too much opposition by the public and by lawmakers. Violating the United States Constitution could also be a problem, of course. For those reasons, the U.S. Department of Education used indirect means to establish a national curriculum—means that would not be easily recognized by lawmakers or the public.

This 2000 progress report submitted to UNESCO also said:

> Officials of the U.S. Department of Education, as well as Presidents Bush and Clinton, have applauded the emergence of [curriculum] standards at the state level and in the various

subject areas, but they understood that any suggestion that these were being imposed by Washington would unleash a political backlash. [p. 12 of the progress report]

In this way the federal Department of Education implied that it disguised the national curriculum that it was imposing. Just to make sure that UNESCO knew that the curriculum standards were actually coming from Washington, however, the report added this statement:

Consciousness is thus growing among U.S. educators that...educational outcomes must now meet not only national but international standards. [p. 15 of the Progress Report]

This statement means that curriculum standards composed by the states were designed to meet both the federal government's curriculum guidelines as well as the goals agreed to in the World Declaration on Education for All and at Dakar. Neither state legislators nor the public knew that their own curriculum standards were being composed to meet the demands of Washington and the demands of international agreements. The U.S. Department of Education succeeded in establishing a *de facto* national curriculum without either the public or most lawmakers knowing it was happening. [See the author's book: *Fed Ed: The New Federal Curriculum and How It's Enforced* (St. Paul: EdWatch, 2002.)]

How, then, did the U.S. Department of Education manage to take over education policy in all fifty states? Following is a brief account of how it happened.

In 1994 Congress passed three revolutionary and interconnected education bills. Those bills were Goals 2000: Educate America Act, the School-to-Work Opportunities Act and the funding bill called HR6. The Democratic Party controlled both houses of Congress as well as the Presidency at that time, which made passage of these revolutionary bills somewhat easier.

The primary policy bill is commonly known as "Goals 2000." Legislators and the public were told that this bill, later to become law, was not all that worrisome because the entire program was "voluntary." States could join the program if they wished, said the bill and its proponents, but states certainly did not need to. Participation was said to be a matter of "local control."

The public and legislators, except for a few insiders, were not told that the 1350 page funding bill, HR6, carried a nasty surprise. HR6 stipulated that if states did not join Goals 2000, they would lose all their federal education money.

One state governor, George Allen of Virginia, was determined to oppose this federal intrusion into state education policy. After meeting with federal education officials, however, even Governor Allen capitulated. The reason all 50 states joined Goals 2000 was not because they thought it was good policy. They joined to avoid losing federal money—about 7% of all K-12 education expenditures. [*National Review*, March 8, 2004, p. 35] One of the realities, therefore, is this—Goals 2000, the cornerstone of the federal takeover of education, was passed under false pretenses. It was sold on the basis of its being "voluntary," but it was actually imposed on the states under the threat of losing their federal education funding.

No Child Left Behind (NCLB) follows the same path. The only reason that all fifty states are "voluntarily" participating in NCLB is because they will lose their federal education money if they do not. President George W. Bush's Undersecretary of Education, Eugene Hickok, underscored this truth when he said:

> "If some people are wondering if we are going to hold states' feet to the fire and enforce this [No Child Left Behind], the answer is 'yes.'"…he said that if it's eventually necessary to withhold education money from the states, "We probably would." [Quoted by David Green, *Sun Spot.net*, December 12, 2002]

Federal funding is used as the enforcement stick for more than just participation in the federal programs. Funding is also used to coerce states into doing what the federal guidelines require. Michael Cohen, President Clinton's Undersecretary of Education, said:

> The odds are pretty high that governors and state legislators in most states will continue to think that they have a free hand in these [NCLB] issues. This means that if the Education Department wants to ensure state compliance with these requirements, it must launch a sustained communication strategy targeted to legislators and governors. The Secretary must explain that, from now on, he is their partner when it comes to testing and accountability…. Assessment systems in California, West Virginia and Alabama were found by the Secretary of Education to be substantially out of compliance…And the states were told they must enter into compliance agreements to remain eligible for Title I funding. [Paper delivered to the Thomas B. Fordham Foundation, February 13, 2002]

This is an amazing statement by Cohen. He essentially said that the state legislators and governors believed the rhetoric about the federal education laws supposedly being matters of "local control." It is now time for a reality-check for governors and state legislators, said Cohen.

The key feature of the federal take-over of education is controlling the curriculum. Curriculum means subject matter. The curriculum of any school is the content of what that school teaches. Controlling the curriculum allows the education radicals to dictate what schools will teach.

The initial mechanism by which the federal Department of Education took over the school curriculum was contained in several small paragraphs contained in the 1994 education funding bill, HR6. The key paragraphs say:

> (1)(A) The Secretary [of Education] is authorized to carry out a program to enhance the third and sixth National Education Goals [of Goals 2000] by educating students about the history and principles of the United States, including the Bill of Rights, and to foster civic competence and responsibility. [Title X, Sec. 10601 a.]

"Carry out a program" by "educating students" means that the federal government is going to insert itself into K-12 education, a field that had always been reserved for state and local government. Keep in mind that the eight National Education Goals were based on the international agreement known as the World Declaration on Education for All. The language above also means, therefore, that the Secretary of Education is now authorized to impose the EFA international agreement on all schools.

HR6 continues by saying:

> (B) Such programs shall be known as "We the People: The Citizen and the Constitution." The programs shall (A) continue and expand the educational activities of the "We the People: The Citizen and the Constitution" program administered by the Center for Civic Education; and (B) enhance student attainment of challenging content standards in civics and government. [Title X, Sec. 10601 a.]

It would be difficult to overstate the enormous significance of these few words. They mean that the Department of Education is now going to set "content standards" for the schools. "Content standards" means curriculum standards. That is, the federal government has now authorized itself to effectively establish the curriculum for the schools.

In addition, the law quoted above stipulates that the curriculum for civics and government will be determined by one non-governmental organization (NGO) known as the Center for Civic Education (CCE). This single NGO was authorized by this law to write the federal government's curriculum standards for civics and government. Incredibly, the law contained no requirement that this civics curriculum even be brought back to Congress for debate or approval! The CCE was given a blank check, which meant that whatever curriculum the CCE constructed would essentially be the actual civics and government curriculum of the United States of America.

HR6 also funded the CCE for accomplishing its task. This funding bill said:

> The Secretary is authorized to award a grant or enter into a contract with the Center for Civic Education to carry out the program described in paragraph (1). [Title X, Section 10601 a.]

The CCE did, in fact, publish its curriculum standards for civics and government and did so in 1994. This curriculum was apparently ready to go before the 1994 funding bill was passed. This was insider politics at its worst. These curriculum standards are called *The National Standards for Civics and Government.* They were published by, and can be purchased from:

Center for Civic Education,
5146 Douglas Fir Road,
Calabasas, CA, 91302-1467
Toll Free (800) 350-4223

The publishers describe the book as follows: "These standards specify what students should know and be able to do in the field of civics and government." "Grades K-12, 1994.187 pages. ISBN 0-89818-155-0."

We must recognize that the members of the CCE never face the voting public. The insider change-agents in the U.S. Department of Education likewise never face the voting public. How ironic it is that at the time of so-called "accountability in education," the people who are writing the curriculum standards are themselves accountable to no one.

By means of the laws described above in this chapter, the U.S. Department of Education has essentially taken control of the schools, including the school curriculum. No one informed lawmakers or the public that the U.S. Department of Education was establishing the curriculum to be used in the schools.

The No Child Left Behind law, enacted in 2002, contains the same language as that contained in HR6. This means that the U.S. Department of Education, along with its inner circle of friends including the CCE, continues to effectively control the curriculum in the schools of the United States.

This federal curriculum now forms the basis for the federal government's own achievement test—the National Assessment of Educational Progress (NAEP). It also forms the basis for most, if not all, the other national achievement tests. The Stanford webpage, for example, says that the new Stanford achievement tests are based on the national curriculum standards (Federal Curriculum). The SAT test is now being revised based on the Federal Curriculum. Most textbooks are now based on the Federal Curriculum as well.

The U.S. Department of Education (DOE) has interpreted the laws above to mean that it has the authority to establish the curriculum in all other subject areas beyond civics and government. The national curriculum standards for mathematics, (NCTM) standards, described in Chapter 2, were seen by the DOE as being authorized by the language quoted above. These are the math standards based on postmodern ideology; the standards that have reduced millions of American children to an inferior academic position from which they are unable to do college-level math.

These national curriculum standards also require the teaching of pantheism (see Chapters 3, 4 & 5). Under the cover of "sustainable development," "environmentalism" and "multiculturalism," the teaching of pantheistic/New Age religion is now required in the national curriculum standards for history, geography, mathematics, civics and government, and language arts.

The events and other factual information contained in this chapter describe a *de facto coup d'etat*. A small group of radicals within the U.S. Department of Education and elsewhere have effectively taken control of the curriculum in our schools. They are now using the American schools to indoctrinate our children with their radical worldviews and to train our children to be political activists on behalf of their extremist political agenda.

The issue before us today is whether the United States can reestablish itself as a free and independent nation governed by the will of the people—or whether we are now ready to give away our freedom and be ruled by the will of the radical few who occupy the inner circle of power here and at the UN. Hopefully, it is not too late to change course. And, yes, it really is this serious.

CHAPTER TWELVE

Global Education

As we have seen, both Goals 2000 and No Child Left Behind were based on the international agreements known as the World Declaration on Education for All, 1990, and the Dakar Framework for Action, 2000. Since President Bush, Sr. and President Clinton committed the United States to implementing these international agreements, we would have reason to be surprised only if the federal education laws had not followed the international accords.

Why is this significant? Why does it matter that our own education policies are now largely the result of international agreements? To answer this question, we will look once more at several of the quotations included in Chapter 11, this time from the perspective of the implications for the United States. We will also consider several other important quotations.

The international connections to our education system are significant for the following eight reasons:

1. The international agreements on education are based on the Marxist worldview of Antonio Gramsci, not the worldview of the free West. The Marxist worldview is centered on three big lies. The first lie is that all history and economics can be explained in terms of the exploitation of the vulnerable by the rich and powerful. By way of analogy, the lie says that the reason some ships are small is because they have been exploited by bigger ships. The second lie is closely related to the first, namely, that all ships must be the same size. The third lie is related to the first two; it says government can manage the tide so that small ships are raised more than big ships. These are the three big lies of Marxism and they are the reason why Marxist socialism does not work.

No Child Left Behind is based on the same three lies. NCLB forces schools to eliminate the disparities between groups rather than raise the achievement levels of everyone. Which would be better—to raise the achievement of all groups by one grade level? Or raise the achievement of the lowest students by one grade level while the achievement of other students remains the same? NCLB forces schools to follow the second approach. This Marxist philosophy has not worked anywhere else. Why should we expect it to work in education?

NCLB assumes that the reason some groups perform below other groups is because of racism in the schools. Is there hard evidence to support that position? No, there is not. In contrast to this lie, the research of Barbara Dafoe Whitehead's research suggests that racial and ethnic differences on achievement tests are primarily the result of family structure, not discrimination. If you adjust for family structure, says Whitehead, the racial and ethnic differences largely disappear. [Barbara Dafoe Whitehead, "Dan Quayle Was Right," *Atlantic*, April, 1993] Unless No Child Left Behind has a way of rebuilding families (it doesn't), it is avoiding the real problem.

As to the details, NCLB requires schools to bring all students up to proficiency levels by the year 2014. It also requires schools to demonstrate "adequate yearly progress" (AYP) toward that goal. (Schools must make it $1/12^{th}$ of the way each year.) Even though the law makes minimal exceptions for special needs students, it still, nonetheless, creates a system where states are motivated to set proficiency requirements so low that they are almost meaningless. If states set proficiency levels at a point where they are meaningful, then the legal requirements of the law will be impossible to meet. Schools that fail to meet the NCLB requirements will be labeled failing schools and are subject to state takeover if they cannot comply.

"Adequate yearly progress" applies only to students below the determined proficiency level. Students above that level are irrelevant to NCLB. For that reason, schools will of necessity draw resources away from average and gifted students, often called "the Robin Hood effect."

NCLB requires schools to show "adequate yearly progress" for not only the student body as a whole, but also for every student subgroup. This means that subgroups identified by race, ethnic background, and economic status must all show "adequate yearly progress." NCLB says the learning gaps represented by these subgroups must be closed by 2014.

Consider, for example, the subgroups of kids coming from an inner city who are characterized by fatherless homes, poverty, high crimes rates, gangs, and English as a second language. What kind of magic-wand do schools have to raise every member of this kind of subgroup up to a high level of academic proficiency? It is one thing to have good schools; it is quite another to require schools to be miracle-workers. The details of NCLB cannot be done.

Why, then has NCLB given us a fantasy-world education system instead of a program that can work? The reason is that it is based on the false worldview of Antonio Gramsci. The reason is that NCLB was designed to meet the objectives of the international agreement known as the Declaration on Education for All and its update at Dakar. Designing a plan that was workable and good for kids was of secondary importance. In addition, people who see themselves as the new Masters cannot imagine that their grandiose plans aren't the best ones possible.

How can our nation actually provide superior educational opportunity for all students? It will not happen by pitting one group against another, but it can happen by following the advice of education expert E. D. Hirsch who has said we should throw out progressive education and go back to the traditional education methods of 40 years ago that actually worked—when SAT scores were 75 points higher than they are today. It can happen by following the principles of genuine academic education as explained in Part II of this book.

2. The American people and most U.S. lawmakers at all levels have been deceived about the nature of our new education system. As noted above, the year 2000 progress report submitted to UNESCO said:

> Most countries have national curricula and even national examinations,…In the United States, however, education is managed at the state and local levels…Thus, the very concept of designing and agreeing on a [national] set of learning outcomes across traditional jurisdictional lines is new, and in the minds of many, unsettling and undesirable. [p. 12 of the U.S. progress report to UNESCO]

The reference above to the creation of "learning outcomes across traditional jurisdictional lines" means that the educational goals are now being formulated by the federal government, not the state and local governments as required by the U.S. Constitution. The writers of the report to UNESCO acknowledged that the American public and lawmakers would object if they knew that the new education system is really being directed by Washington.

Also as quoted above, the 2000 progress report submitted to UNESCO said:

> Officials of the U.S. Department of Education, as well as Presidents Bush and Clinton, have applauded the emergence of [curriculum] standards at the state level and in the various subject areas, but they understood that any suggestion that these were being imposed by Washington would unleash a political backlash. [p. 12 of the progress report to UNESCO]

Most of these state education curriculum standards were based on the Federal Curriculum standards. The Minnesota Department of Education website, for example, used to say that the state curriculum standards were based on the national curriculum standards (Federal Curriculum). Just to make sure that UNESCO understood that the state curriculum standards were based on the national curriculum standards, the report to UNESCO added this clarification:

> Consciousness is thus growing among U.S. educators that...educational outcomes must now meet not only national but international standards. [P.15 of the Progress Report to UNESCO]

The objectives of the education systems at the state and local levels now have to meet the objectives specified at the national level and at the international level. Teachers and lawmakers are only just beginning to understand what has happened. The point is that the nation's lawmakers and the public were deceived about the actual nature of the federal education laws. Laws based on deception are bad laws.

3. States are being forced to participate in the new education system for the wrong reasons. Are states participating in No Child Left Behind because they believe it is good for the education of their children? Not at all. The reason all fifty states are participating was explained by Michael Cohen, President Clinton's Undersecretary of Education, who, as we observed previously, said:

> The odds are pretty high that governors and state legislators in most states will continue to think that they have a free hand in these [NCLB] issues. This means that if the Education Department wants to ensure state compliance with these requirements, it must launch a sustained communication

strategy targeted to legislators and governors. The Secretary must explain that, from now on, he is their partner when it comes to testing and accountability.... Assessment systems in California, West Virginia and Alabama were found by the Secretary of Education to be substantially out of compliance.... And the states were told they must enter into compliance agreements to remain eligible for Title I funding. [Michael Cohen, Paper delivered to the Thomas B. Fordham Foundation, February 2, 2002.]

Michael Cohen was responsible for setting up the new federal education system under President Bill Clinton. He knows what he is talking about. He pointed out that governors and state legislators had been misled regarding the federal government's new role in education policy. He also makes it crystal clear that states are being coerced into compliance with the new system by the threat of the withholding of federal funding. States are not participating in the federal (and international) system because they believe the program is good for their kids. They are participating because they want the federal money.

4. The making of major education policy decisions at the United Nations involves a significant movement toward international decision-making as opposed to national and state decision-making. The question, of course, is: Do we want global governance or do we want state and national governance? One modestly encouraging sign on this crucial question is that one member of the Bush cabinet has begun to speak out about the dangers of global governance. Labor Secretary Elaine Chao was recently reported as having said:

President Bush's labor secretary warned a gathering of conservatives that Americans must pay more attention to the United Nations and its related organizations, which she noted were chipping away at U.S. sovereignty and freedoms. Labor Secretary Elaine Chao...explained that powerful tax-exempt organizations were applying pressure to the UN to have the world body make decisions for Americans' lives without any input from U.S. citizens.... And, she fears, "one day the U.S. will be pressured to accept" the globalist agenda without a single vote being cast. [NewsMax.com, January 23, 2004]

Elaine Chao has identified the central issue in the international education agenda. It is the question of national sovereignty and freedom versus global governance.

Citizens in Minnesota have been in the middle of this battle as it relates to Minnesota's education standards. Because of extensive citizen involvement in education issues, Minnesota became the first state in the Union to throw out the Federal Curriculum. It did so in the spring of 2003. In 2003 and 2004 Minnesota adopted new state curriculum standards.

Following the lead of citizen writing committees created by law in 2003, the Republican-controlled Minnesota House proposed curriculum standards that gave national sovereignty a prominent place in the curriculum standards for social studies. The standards proposed by the Democrat-controlled Senate, in contrast, removed "national sovereignty" from the teaching requirements. The Democrat-controlled Senate, which works closely with the Center for Civic Education, wanted national sovereignty to be out of sight and out of mind.

What, then, did the Democrat bill substitute in place of national sovereignty? The curriculum requirements developed by the Democrats never used the word "national sovereignty" even once, but they did use the word "global" 32 times! This imbalance tells the whole story on the issue of sovereignty. The imbalance means that the Democratic leadership in Minnesota, under the guidance of the CCE, wants Minnesota kids to think of government in global terms, not in terms of a national government that is sovereign and free.

When the House and Senate bills went to conference committee, there was only one issue that the Democrat-controlled Senate refused to reconsider—that was the issue of including national sovereignty in the curriculum requirements. The Republicans were able to make substantial progress on other issues related to the state standards, but the Senate would not budge on national sovereignty. By their actions the Democrats in the Minnesota Senate made it crystal clear that **eliminating national sovereignty was for them the one central and critical issue in the new system of education.**

It is also the central issue in the international education agreements. The issue is national freedom and sovereignty versus global governance. This is also the central issue in the federal curriculum—the issue of teaching our children to be citizens of a United States that is free, versus teaching them to be political activists on behalf of world federalism.

5. The international agreements have given us an education system which promotes integrated math, postmodernism, pantheism, new Marxism and world government. These central themes are described and documented elsewhere. Integrated math is described in Chapter 2. For postmodernism see Chapter 3. Pantheism is explained in Chapters 6, 7 and 8. New Marxism is detailed in Chapter 4. For world government, see Chapter13. Promotion of these radical themes is a matter of indoctrination, not academic education. This is transformational education designed to indoctrinate our kids in ideology, politics and religion. It is not academic education.

6. The international agreements have given us achievement tests that are invalid. Our national tests are now testing the ideological themes listed above as opposed to focusing on legitimate academic achievement. Regarding the federal government's test in mathematics, for example, the federal agency known as McREL said:

> The influence of the NCTM Standards [is that it provided the]...framework for the National Assessment of Educational Progress [NAEP]. [http://www.mcrel.org/Standards-bench-marks/ docs/history.asp, p. 1]

Since the NAEP test, as well as other tests, is now based on integrated math as opposed to traditional math, we no longer have a valid measure on how well our students are learning math. As a consequence, it will be very difficult, if not impossible, to compare the math achievement of our students today to the achievement of students in the past or to the achievement of students in other countries. The only comparisons we will have will come from the colleges and universities. They will continue to tell us that students schooled in integrated math are unable to do college-level mathematics.

7. The international agreements have caused an end-run around or violation of the U.S. Constitution. The Tenth Amendment to the U.S. Constitution makes it clear that education is a governmental function that is reserved for states, local governments, and the people. NCLB violates, or, at minimum is an "end run" around this constitutional principle.

The Tenth Amendment is in our Constitution for a reason. That reason results from the conviction of our forefathers that it was dangerous to allow too much political power to become centralized in one place. Violating the Tenth Amendment has produced exactly what our nation's founders were afraid of—the centralizing of governmental power at Washington D.C. and, worse yet, at the United Nations. The farther away this power is from the citizens, the more difficult it is for the people to change it. Abraham Lincoln said our government was created to be a government "of the people, by the people, and for the people." Lincoln's accurate and lofty description pictures a government that exists in a world far removed from the new international system of education.

8. The purpose of the international education system is hostile to the freedom and sovereignty of the United States. American lawmakers and the American public need to recognize the real agenda of the international education agreements. What is that agenda? R. Freeman Butts, Senior Advisor for the Center for Civic Education, described the purpose of the international education agreements. In a speech called "Viewed from Afar: A New Meaning for World-Class Standards in Education," R. Freeman Butts said:

> Comenius antedated our contemporary calls for world-class standards by proposing an outlook called pansophism, i.e., **teaching a common body of universal knowledge to all children everywhere** that could pave the road to universal peace in a war-torn world. He envisioned a **universal system of schools** in which the whole human race could be educated, including all ages, all social classes, both sexes, and all nations: a truly universal education (panpaedia)...[Emphasis added; presented at <u>CIVITAS@PRAGUE.1995.</u>]

Butts is quoting Comenius approvingly. As seen from the quotation, Comenius called for a "common body of universal knowledge" – a common world curriculum. Is that what the international agreements are all about? The NEA has clearly thought so. When UNESCO was formed, the NEA journal said:

> The establishment of [UNESCO] marks the culmination of a movement for the creation of an international agency for education which began with Comenius.... Nations that become members of UNESCO accordingly assume an obligation to revise the textbooks used in their schools...[I. L. Kandel, *NEA Journal*, 1946]

This NEA article stated that the purpose of UNESCO is the creation of a world curriculum developed by an international agency as promoted by Comenius. In addition, in 1957 UNESCO identified Comenius to be its "spiritual father."

Why should we have a common world curriculum? The Malaysia education website included an article (posted in 2001, but no longer available) which described the new international system of education. The Malaysia website said:

The global village requires a...common curriculum [which is the]...international component in the educational system....

That is, according to the article on the Malaysia education website, the reason for establishing a world curriculum is the creation of the "global village." (The new Federal Curriculum aggressively advocates the global village. See Chapter 14.) Those who have followed UNESCO over the years know that the creation of the global village has always been UNESCO's ultimate goal. This UN organization was more open about its primary objective when it was new. In 1949, for example, UNESCO said:

[Children should be taught] those qualities of citizenship which provide the foundation upon which international government must be based if it is to succeed. [UNESCO pamphlet published in 1949]

Along the same lines, the first Director-General of UNESCO, Sir Julian Huxley said:

Specifically, in its educational program it [UNESCO] can stress the ultimate need for world political unity and familiarize all peoples with the implications of the transfer of full sovereignty from separate nations to a world organization...political unification in some sort of world government will be required. [Sir Julian Huxley, *UNESCO: Its Purpose and Philosophy*, 1947, p. 13]

The purpose of UNESCO is, of course, no different from the purpose of the United Nations. And what is the purpose of the UN? Secretary General Kofi Annan was described by *Time* during the UN Millennium Summit as follows:

Annan's speech was almost always the same, a reasoned and moving pitch for global community.... Annan is a committed globalist. [*Time*, September 4, 2000, p. 39]

The United Nation's own publishing house leaves little room for doubt about the way it sees itself. In its book *Global Governance and the United Nations System*, the UN described its mission as follows:

In 1998 we started work on the subproject "Global Governance and the United Nations" and tried to determine how the UN system might cope with the apparent need for institutional adaptation and reform. The starting point of the research was the fundamental change in the global system. The end of the cold war and the bipolar system, on the one hand, and the growing number of resourceful private actors in the international arena—such as transnational corporations (TNCs) or non-governmental organizations (I/NGOs)—on the other, **point to a beginning of the end of the (Westphalian) international system with its territorially rooted borderlines and nation-states.** [emphasis added, *Global Governance and the United Nations* (New York: 2001, United Nations University Press) p. ix]

The UN has certainly made its position crystal clear. Its leadership believes that nations and national boundaries are obsolete and must be replaced with a new governmental order. This new world order is identified in the title of its book—*Global Governance and the United Nations.* The UN intends to be the global government. The UN describes what it believes the new world order should look like with statements like the following:

The main focus of this volume is the prospect of global governance based on the UN system. [*Ibid.* p. x]

The concept of citizenship is being transformed... [*Ibid.* p. 8]

Nation states have lost their position as the paramount loci of governance...[*Ibid.* p 17]

A world republic would be governed by a federal world government. [*Ibid.* p 26]

Only a federalist unity can be morally dictated and a legitimate world republic. As a consequence, all power of the world state comes from its democratic legitimacy...from the community of all human beings and from all states. [*Ibid.* p. 198]

The world state...would be a federalist world republic. [*Ibid.* p. 199]

Last but not least, the UN Charter amounts to nothing less than a world Constitution. [*Ibid.* p. 200]

> The United Nations has been founded by sovereign states. However, by the ratification of the Charter, they renounced part of their sovereignty and headed towards a federal world republic. [*Ibid.* p. 200]

The thesis of this UN publication is that world government, under UN command, will come; the only question is what form this world government should take. The leadership of the UN is committed to world government, federalist or otherwise, and they intend to do everything they can to move this agenda along. The American public, of course, has no idea what the real purpose of the UN and its branch organization, UNESCO, actually is today.

The UN's goal of world government is right in line with the thinking of the former Clinton administration. One of Bill Clinton's closest friends, former roommate and top advisor, Strob Talbot, said:

> In the next century national sovereignty as we know it will be obsolete. All states will recognize a single global authority. [Strob Talbot, *Time*, July 20, 1992]

The World Federalist Society gave Talbot an award for his pro-world government comments. President Bill Clinton responded by sending Talbot a congratulatory letter and by appointing him to the number two position in the U. S. State Department. How likely is it that Talbot was looking out for the interests of the United States in that post?

The U.S. Department of Education is largely run by the same world government crowd that governs the UN. For example, the Department of Education lists the Communitarian Network as one of its "Partners in Education." The Communitarian Network Platform, included on its webpage, clarifies that it is dedicated to world government. In addition, under the lead of the Department of Education, the United States rejoined UNESCO several months ago after having formally left the organization during the Reagan Presidency.

Why, again, can the Utah grade-school girl no longer succeed in math? The answer is at Dakar. The answer is at UNESCO. The answer is at the UN. The answer is in the inner-circle of power in our international world that has much bigger goals to consider than whether grade-school kids in America can do math.

There is always the possibility, of course, that this inner-circle of power does not want grade-school kids in America to be able to do math.

CHAPTER THIRTEEN

Targeting the United States

In its book *Enhancing Global Governance*, the United Nations University Press explains its perceived obstacles in creating a world government centered at the UN. The book says that even though it was an American President–Woodrow Wilson and his proposed League of Nations–that began the road to global government, it is ironically now the United States that is world government's biggest obstacle.

The Presidency of Ronald Reagan was an enormous setback to global government, says this book. This UN publication laments:

> Under Reagan, so complete was the collapse of support for the institutions of global governance in the USA that a 1995 article in *Foreign Policy* announced the "twilight of internationalism." [*Enhancing Global Governance* (New York: United Nations University Press, 2002) p. 63]

The UN publication also says:

> To a Wilsonian or FDR liberal, the 1980s may have witnessed the "twilight of internationalism," but to Reagan and neo-conservatives it was "morning in America"—an exquisitely beautiful sunrise over God's Own Country that held all the promise for the world. Reagan's concept of American exceptionalism was vintage 17th century, and the triumphalism attendant on the end of the Cold war served to reinforce this pre-modern strain in American thinking. [*Ibid.* p. 64]

The internationalists writing this book are adamantly opposed to "morning in America," of course, and they saw Reagan as an evolutionary throwback to the 17th century. But the internationalists, observes this book, were much more hopeful when Bill Clinton was elected President. Clinton, however, was effectively hemmed in by the Republican landslide in the Congressional elections of 1994. The Republican control of Congress, says this UN book, prevented much of the anticipated increase of support for world governance in the United States even though the President was "like minded" with the globalists.

The UN sees the election of George W. Bush to the Presidency as another obstacle for world governance. *Enhancing Global Governance* says:

> Looking ahead, from the perspective of the UN system it is not easy to contemplate the administration of George W. Bush without experiencing a premonition of trouble. A columnist for the *New York Times* has observed that, "your average TWA pilot knows more about the world than George W. Bush", but the root problem is apparently a deep-seated antipathy to international organizations and mechanisms of global governance on the part of the new Republican administration. [*Ibid.* p. 67]

What to do? According to *Enhancing Global Governance*, the United States is the significant barrier to global government, and George W. Bush, who is not "like-minded," is now President of the United States. How can the UN accomplish its global governance goals? The answer to this question, argues the UN's book, is in this observation:

> ...it was the British historian James Bryce, long-time ambassador to Washington, who identified public opinion as the key to American government, and laid bare its essential morphology....In the American community, Bryce concluded in an analysis which holds up today, "Public opinion can with truth be said not only to reign but to govern." [*Ibid.* p. 69]

Since the United States is seen by the UN as the significant obstacle to world government, and since public opinion is viewed as "the key" to government policy in the United States, it makes all the sense in the world for the UN to target public opinion in the United States. That is what the international education system is all about—indoctrinating the children of the United States with the ideological building blocks for supporting world government. The next chapter will continue to explain how this indoctrination is taking place.

One question needs to be answered before proceeding, however—if President Bush is opposed to world government, why is he supporting No Child Left Behind? There are two reasons. The first was his hope that by supporting NCLB, he would cut into the Democrats' political advantage on the education issue. *National Review* explained the Bush strategy as follows:

> When George W. Bush hit the campaign trail in 2000, Republicans ranked 20 points behind Democrats on which party best handled the issue of education. In 2002, Republicans were delighted to find that that deficit had vanished—thanks to President Bush's advocacy for his land-mark education reform plan, No Child Left Behind. Today, however, Democrats once again enjoy a double-digit advantage on education issues, and the plan's bipartisan support didn't survive the Iowa caucuses. [*National Review*, March 8, 2004, p. 35]

The second reason President Bush and his top administrators support NCLB is they fail to understand the radical nature of its hidden curriculum. They know little, if anything, about integrated math, postmodernism, pantheism/New Age religion, world federalism, and the new Marxism which permeate the Federal Curriculum. In addition, the Bush team has no idea that NCLB is America's plan for implementing Dakar. At a town meeting in Burnsville, Minnesota, Undersecretary of Education Eugene Hickok was asked how the United States was implementing the Dakar agreement. He answered by saying that he did not know. Hickok also said that he knew virtually nothing about the Dakar Action Plan itself.

This kind of ignorance regarding the federal education system is, unfortunately, typical of Republican administrations. George Bush and his associates did not design No Child Left Behind. It was constructed by inner-circle Democrats and like-minded bureaucrats within the Department of Education. The details of NCLB were planned out by Bill Clinton and his like-minded world government friends, not by the Republicans. *Enhancing Global Governance* says:

> The U.S.A. is not, finally a "like-minded country" [supportive of world government]…but it contains many like-minded institutions and like-minded people. [*Enhancing Global Governance*, p. 67]

These "like-minded people" and "like-minded institutions" are associates of Bill Clinton and John Kerry, not George Bush. The "like-minded people" are the individuals who have designed the new federal education system. The "like-minded people," however, have camouflaged their program well. Democrats are shrewder than Republicans, especially when it comes to promoting their ideology. When Bill Clinton was elected President in 1992, he made sure that his people were in total control of all the state departments of the federal government. The code language for these individuals is "like-minded people" and "like-minded institutions" including the Center for Civic Education, the Communitarian Network, the environmental groups, and many others.

Republicans generally do not govern the same way. Republicans appoint trusted people as the secretaries of the state departments, but they only partially replace the next level of administrators. As a consequence, the bureaucrats, who in the Department of Education at least are like-minded with Bill Clinton, still run the show.

In this reality, however, comes reason for real hope. If we, the citizens of America, can succeed in informing the American people and the Republican leadership about the true nature of the new international education system and about the nature of the bureaucracy that is running it, perhaps the Republican leadership will then begin to turn it around.

CHAPTER FOURTEEN

Review of
We the People: The Citizen and the Constitution

How is world government actually being taught by the federal education system in the schools of United States? The building blocks of world government are being taught in numerous ways. This chapter explains how world government is being taught in one high school textbook. This text is the only one authorized and funded by federal law. It is the only text which is officially part of the federal takeover of education. It is the textbook called *We The People: The Citizen And The Constitution*. This book was first authorized and funded in HR6, 1994, and was re-authorized and funded in No Child Left Behind, 2002. This book is the Federal Curriculum for civics and government in textbook form. The language in NCLB which reauthorized and refunded the textbook reads as follows:

Sec 2344. *We The People Program*
(a) THE CITIZEN AND THE CONSTITUTION.—
(1) EDUCATIONAL ACTIVITIES.—The Center for Civic Education—
(A) shall use funds made available under grants or contracts under section 2343(a)(1)—...(iii) to provide a course of instruction on the basic principles of our Nation's constitutional democracy and the history of the Constitution of the United States including the Bill of Rights....

We The People: The Citizen And The Constitution is published by the Center for Civic Education, 5146 Douglas Fir Road, Calabasas, CA, 91302-1467, 818-591-9321, http://www.civiced.org. The copyright date is 1995; seventh printing is dated 2000, 283 pages. At this time the book lists for $12.00. ($10.00 for quantities of ten or more.) This book is the least expensive civics textbook available, the reason being that it is subsidized by tax dollars.

Several important questions should be considered regarding the publishing of this text. Why, for example, should the federal government be involved in authorizing and subsidizing the publishing of a high-school textbook? Other textbooks are neither authorized nor subsidized; why should this one be?

Second, if the federal government is to subsidize a textbook, why shouldn't it give various companies or organizations the opportunity to bid on the project? Why should federal law specify that one and only one organization is authorized, at taxpayer expense, to publish a textbook?

And third, we notice not only that one NGO (non-governmental organization) was authorized and funded to write this textbook, we also notice that Congress has not established a review process. How will Congress know if the Center for Civic Education (CCE) has written an acceptable textbook? The obvious implication of these three questions is this: The authorizing and funding of this textbook is the result of insider politics at its worst. We shouldn't be surprised if there is a political agenda of some kind in this textbook.

POSTMODERNISM

The postmodernist philosophy of this book is one of its most prominent features. The text, for example, consistently treats our foundational principles as "ideas," but never as "truths." The textbook, for example, states:

> This unit provides an overview of some important philosophical **ideas** and historic events that influenced the writing of our Constitution and the Bill of Rights. The first and second lessons in this unit introduce you to some basic **ideas** of the natural rights **philosophy** and **theories** of government. These **ideas** were of great importance in the development of our government. The remaining lessons in this unit examine in greater detail the historical background of these **ideas**. [emphasis added, p. 1]

There is nothing wrong with describing our foundational principles as ideas, of course. They are ideas. The question is, are these foundational principles **only** ideas, or are they something more? How does our Declaration of Independence, for example, describe its foundational

90

principles? It does so by calling our foundation principles "self-evident truths," not mere "ideas." Calling these principles "truths" says much more than just calling them "ideas."

In direct contrast to the Declaration of Independence, the only time *We The People, The Citizen And The Constitution* uses the word "truth," is in the Appendix (the Declaration of Independence itself) and when referring to a woman by the name of "Sojourner Truth."

In the spring of 2004, the state of Minnesota adopted new curriculum standards for social studies. The new Minnesota standards specifically clarify that the principles of our nation's founding are self-evident truths, not mere ideas. The Democratic-controlled Senate, in contrast, following the leadership of the Center for Civic Education, wanted our foundational principles treated as mere ideas. The issue was postmodernism versus the traditional view of truth and knowledge. On this critical issue, the Republican-controlled House prevailed—apparently making Minnesota the first state in the union to return to teaching genuine truth as it relates to our foundational principles. The CCE position, in contrast, as clarified in its textbook, is that our foundational principles are philosophy only, not truth.

In the last chapter, the CCE textbook further explains its postmodernist position. The textbook says:

> As fundamental and lasting as its guarantees have been [past tense], the U.S. Bill of Rights is a document of the eighteenth century, reflecting the issues and concerns of the age in which it was written.... Other national guarantees of rights also reflect the cultures that created them. Many of these cultures have values and priorities different from our own. In many Asian countries, for example, the rights of the individuals are secondary to the interests of the whole community. Islamic countries take their code of laws from the teachings of the Koran, the book of sacred writings accepted by Muslims as revelations to the prophet Mohammad by God. [p. 207]

In other words, the text views our Bill of Rights as merely a creation of our culture while other forms of government are creations of their cultures. This is standard dogma for postmodernists. To them, there are no truths, just "constructs" formulated by cultures.

The way postmodernists see it, no form of national government is better than others, none is worse; all cultures and their creations are equal. Postmodernists view our foundational principles as being belief statements of a particular culture at a particular time. According to postmodernists, the principles of national sovereignty, natural law and the natural rights of life, liberty and property may have been useful for the culture that embraced them 200 years ago, but that does not mean these principles are appropriate for us today. Postmodernism rejects the position that "self-evident truths" and "unalienable rights" formed the foundation of our nation.

It is especially significant to observe that while this textbook consistently presents our nation's foundational principles as mere ideas, postmodernism, in contrast, is never presented as being only an idea or philosophy. Postmodernism is always presented as being true. The textbook mirrors the inherent contradiction of postmodernism which says that all truths are social constructs except those held by postmodernism.

This distinction between real truth and postmodernism comprises a primary paradigm shift between traditional, academic education and the new, radical system of education. People who do not recognize this paradigm shift, including many lawmakers, are easily misled into believing the national standards are saying something they are not.

At the same time, however, everyone must take some position regarding the question of what is true. Compare, for example, the way this textbook treats human rights, as defined by our Declaration of Independence, to the manner in which it describes the UN's Universal Declaration of Human Rights. When describing the latter document, the textbook says:

> The social, economic, and **solidarity rights** included in the United Nations' Universal Declaration of Human Rights, and in many national guarantees of rights adopted since, are what are sometimes called **positive rights**.... positive rights...describe certain benefits that citizens should have. These rights express the objectives worthy of any just society. [textbook's emphasis, p. 208]

Notice the attitude the textbook takes toward the UN's Universal Declaration of Human Rights. The UN's Declaration is not viewed as being merely one culture's ideas at one point in time. Not at all. The UN's Declaration is described as being "worthy" of "any just society." It is described in terms that are absolute and universal, not in terms relative to culture. The intent is to make the Universal Declaration of Human Rights appear to be superior to our own Bill of Rights.

The text never points out, of course, that the Universal Declaration of Human Rights takes the same form as the statements of rights in the constitutions of all Communist countries. The UN Declaration of

Human Rights ends with the words: "These rights and freedoms may in no case be exercised contrary to the purposes and principles of the United Nations." That is, the UN policies must come first; individual human rights come second—in contradistinction to the Declaration of Independence which insists that inalienable human rights have a higher priority than government decisions.

Consistent with its postmodernist worldview, *We The People: The Citizen And The Constitution* takes a dim view of teaching factual information. The text says:

> The primary purpose of this textbook is not to fill your head with a lot of facts about American history and government. Knowledge of the facts is important but only in so far as it deepens your understanding of the American constitutional system and its development. [p. X]

That is, the proper "understanding of the American constitutional system" (as defined by the postmodernist ideology of the textbook) is the filter that determines which facts will be taught and which facts will be ignored. Facts are de-emphasized. "Historical thinking" becomes the goal of education, not the attaining of historical knowledge.

Content of the Textbook

As noted above, the textbook says that it intends to teach the proper "understanding of the American constitutional system." That statement is the filter which determines which facts are presented and which are omitted. We will allow the textbook to explain this operating principle by observing how it answers the following four specific questions:

1. What is *We The People*'s view of the Bill of Rights?
2. What is *We The People*'s view of each of the first ten amendments which make up the Bill of Rights?
3. What is *We The People*'s view of national sovereignty?
4. What is *We The People*'s view of foundational principles?

The answers to these four questions will be sufficient to determine what is meant by the book's definition of "understanding of the American constitutional system":

1. What is *We The People*'s view of the Bill of Rights?

In addition to its overall postmodernist philosophy, *We The People: The Citizen And The Constitution* expresses its attitude toward the Bill of Rights this way:

The reaction of most people to the Bill of Rights was **luke-warm at best**. Its passage had **little effect on the average person**....The Anti-Federalists, who had based much of their opposition to the Constitution on the lack of a bill of rights, **were unhappy with its passage**. They thought it **spoiled their chances** to rewrite the Constitution. They said the amendments were **"good for nothing."** "I believe," said Senator William Grayson of Virginia, "as many others do, **they will do more harm than good**." At the same time, **Federalists were angry** with Madison for pushing the Bill of Rights through Congress. **At best, they considered it of little importance**. Even Madison, **tired of all the disagreement and dissent**, had come to think of the **whole experience as a "nauseous project."** [emphasis added, p. 100]

As can be seen from this statement, the textbook's view of the Bill of Rights is decidedly negative.

2. What is *We The People*'s attitude toward the first ten Amendments which make up the Bill of Rights?

Units 1 through 4 of the textbook describe the historical development of our system of government up to the present time. Unit 5 then describes our government as it exists today. Unit 5 is titled "What Rights Does the Bill of Rights Protect?" (Notice the present tense of the verb.) As the title states, this unit describes the basic human rights which are protected by our Constitution today. The following table describes which of our basic rights are supposedly protected by the Constitution today, as well as the number of pages in Unit 5 devoted to each fundamental human right:

"What Rights does the Bill of Rights Protect?"

Number of pages Unit 5 devotes to each Amendment:

First Amendment	16
Second Amendment	0
Third Amendment	1
Amendments Four through Eight	17
Ninth Amendment	0
Tenth Amendment	0

Notice that in this unit the Second, Ninth and Tenth Amendments are never mentioned. Look at the contrast. There are 16 pages of text devoted to the First Amendment, but not one word on the Second. Similarly, there is not one word on the Ninth and Tenth Amendments. These three amendments are viewed as being either nonexistent or unimportant for our day. They are out of sight and out of mind.

The Second Amendment (right to bear arms) was mentioned in the earlier historical development section of the text, but there it was included only under the heading of controversial issues, and the emphasis was on gun control, not the right to bear arms. In addition, the Second Amendment was inaccurately defined as being the right of states to have a militia, not as a personal right to own and bear arms.

What, then, is this textbook's attitude toward the Second Amendment? Its attitude is that the right to bear arms is of historical interest only; that it has always been controversial; that there is a need for more gun control; that the Second Amendment has never meant the right of private citizens to own and bear arms; and that there is no right to bear arms today. This radical political position of eliminating the right to bear arms is an important part of the new Federal Curriculum.

The Ninth and Tenth Amendments are also excluded from this Unit. The Ninth and Tenth Amendments describe the doctrine of "reserved rights." That is, the Ninth Amendment states that individual rights not delegated to the federal government by the Constitution are reserved, or retained, by the people; and the Tenth says that rights not delegated to the federal government by the Constitution are retained by the states or the people, respectively.

In the historical development section of the book, the Ninth Amendment is described in passing, but the Tenth Amendment is never mentioned anywhere in the text of this book. It has been censored out.

Textbooks in American government have always differentiated between the "delegated powers," those given to the federal government, and the "reserved powers," those powers that remain with the states and the people. This textbook uses the term "delegated powers" several times, but it never uses the counterpart term "reserved powers." In this textbook there are no rights reserved to the states or to the people. All rights reside with the federal government.

How can a textbook teach the meaning of constitutional government without teaching the Ninth and Tenth Amendments? It cannot be done. And how can a text teach the doctrine of limited government under our Constitution without teaching the Ninth and Tenth Amendments? It cannot be done. How can a text teach what federalism is without teaching the Tenth Amendment? Again, it cannot be done. According to this textbook, all 50 states and all our citizens are at the mercy of the federal government.

By ignoring the Tenth Amendment, *We The People: The Citizen And The Constitution* teaches the radical view of human rights—the view that human rights are not inalienable, that human rights consist only of those rights that the change-agents wish to include at any point in time and that protecting human rights is not the primary purpose of government. The intent of this textbook is to undermine our free system of government, not to promote it.

3. What is *We The People's* view of National Sovereignty?

We The People: The Citizen And The Constitution asks this question: "What were the main ideas and arguments of the Declaration?" It then answers the question with the following list (p. 45):

1. *Natural law*
2. *Social contract theory*
3. *The purpose of government*
4. *Tyranny of the King of England*
5. *State sovereignty*

Is this list an adequate answer to the question, "What were the main ideas and arguments of the Declaration"? Look at what is missing. The Declaration of Independence itself begins by saying:

> When in the Course of human Events, it becomes necessary for one People to dissolve the Political Bands which have connected them with another, and to assume among the Powers of the Earth, the separate and equal Station to which the Laws of Nature and Nature's God entitle them....

That is, the Declaration of Independence begins with a declaration of national sovereignty. In fact, the Declaration of Independence could just as well be called the "Declaration of National Sovereignty." The meaning is the same. The text of this book, however, never mentions national sovereignty. Not even once. Not even in passing. Not even as a matter of historical interest. National sovereignty is out of sight and out of mind. The text promotes a political agenda which is hostile to national sovereignty.

What is that agenda? Chapter 37 of the textbook has the title, "How May Citizenship Change in the Nation's Third Century?" The chapter begins with the heading called, "Purpose of Lesson," which reads as follows:

This lesson looks to the future. You focus on some major developments taking place in our society that are likely to affect the very nature of citizenship during your lifetime. When you complete this lesson, you should be able to explain how the increased diversity of our society...and closer international relationships are likely to affect your life as a citizen. You should be able to describe how diversity has challenged our civic culture...and how our nation's greater interdependence with the rest of the world is changing the pattern of civic loyalties. [p. 200]

The chapter also states:

Although national citizenship is likely to remain fundamentally important in the future, the issues confronting American citizens are increasingly **international**. Issues of economic competition, the environment, and the movement of peoples around the world require an awareness of political associations that are larger in scope than the nation-state. [textbook's emphasis, p. 202]

What are these "political associations that are larger in scope than the nation-state?" The textbook further explains by saying:

The achievements of modern technology are turning the world into a **global village**. [textbook's emphasis, p. 202]

The chapter then ends with the following question:

What advantages might be offered by world citizenship? What disadvantages? Do you think that world citizenship will be possible in our lifetime? [p. 203]

"Global village" and "world citizenship" mean world government. This text wishes to eliminate national sovereignty and replace it with one-world government. That is the agenda of the book. It is really quite explicit.

The text is not a genuine study of American government at all, nor is the book intended to be educational as we have traditionally defined education in our nation. The book is really propaganda. It is social engineering, not education. It is decidedly anti-American and anti-freedom. It is designed to indoctrinate our citizens into being willing to give away our national sovereignty and freedom and to accept the establishment of world government, instead.

This is how some of the indoctrination proceeds. The text says:

> The achievements of modern technology are turning the world into a **global village**. [textbook's emphasis, p. 202]

The teacher's guide tells the instructors to be sure the students know what the "global village" is. The textbook, however, never defines the term. The term never appears in the glossary. What is the global village? The text never defines the term directly. It does define the term indirectly, however. This is what the book says (pp. 202-203):

> National concerns have become international.

> Environmental concerns also transcend national boundaries.

> The culture we live in is becoming **cosmopolitan**, that is, belonging to the whole world. [textbook's emphasis]

> ...the issues confronting American citizens are increasingly **international**. [textbook's emphasis]

What is the global village? Keep in mind that this is a textbook in government. What happens when we fill in the blanks? The message then is as follows:

- Just as "national concerns have become international," so also government should become international.
- Just as environmental concerns "transcend national boundaries," so also government should transcend national boundaries.
- Just as culture "belongs to the whole world," so also government should belong to the whole world.

Just as "the issues confronting American citizens are increasingly international," so also government needs to become international.

The "global village" is world government. This battle, once again, is exactly the same as the one in 2004 when Minnesota revised its state social studies standards. The proposed standards of the Republican-controlled house made it clear that national sovereignty was to be taught as one of the foundational principles of our nation as stated in the Declaration of Independence. The proposed teaching requirements of the Democratic-controlled Senate, in contrast, never mentioned national sovereignty, but they did use the words "global" or "globalism" 32 times. When push came to shove in conference committee, the Democratic-controlled Senate absolutely refused to budge and include national sovereignty. Everything else was negotiable, but not national sovereignty. Sad to say, the Republican-controlled House finally concluded that it had to accept the new standards without national sovereignty. If those of us in Minnesota ever had any doubts about where the real battle is, our experience in revising our state education standards has removed all doubt.

As clarified above, we are speaking of the battle of ideas. It is actually much more than that, however. It is really the battle for freedom. It is the battle for America— in our schools.

4. What is *We The People*'s view of fundamental principles?

We will now consider how the textbook ends. The last chapter of the book is called: "What is Meant by Returning to Fundamental Principles?" Notice that the chapter is **not** called "Returning to Fundamental Principles." Instead, the chapter is called, "What is **Meant by** Returning to Fundamental Principles?" [emphasis added]

We know what our founding fathers meant by "fundamental principles." Our founding fathers referred to such principles as being "self-evident truths" and "unalienable rights." Is this what *We The People* means by "fundamental principles"? Not at all. "Returning to fundamental principles" is defined by the text as follows:

> It is doubtful that these Founders had in mind an uncritical acceptance of the "wisdom of the past." In revisiting these principles, each generation must examine and evaluate them anew. Indeed, it is probable that the Founders would be somewhat surprised at the reverence in which they and their writings have been held by subsequent generations of Americans.

The textbook continues by saying:

> The Founders, themselves, were vigorous critics of the wisdom they inherited and the principles in which they believed. They were articulate, opinionated individuals who loved to examine ideas, to analyze, argue and debate them. They expected no less of future generations. They would expect no less of you. [p. 214]

As we observed earlier, in this textbook there are no "self-evident truths" which serve as the basis for our nation. There are no "unalienable rights." In this textbook all our basic principles are to be "examined anew." Indeed, our "fundamental principles" are redefined by this text as being a "revisiting" of the fundamental principles upon which our nation was founded. Everything is now up for grabs. According to the textbook, we can observe what the founders of our nation believed, but then was then, and now is now. Every fundamental principle is subject to question. Our nation's fundamental principles are turned on their heads. Every fundamental principle can now be sacrificed for the new fundamental principle of world government. This is what revisionist history becomes. This is what is meant by "constructing history" as is being done by the CCE.

All the while, the CCE, by force of federal law, at taxpayer expense, defines for all Americans what real truth is. The goal of education under the federal takeover is now the "improvement of society" as defined by the CCE. Education has become social engineering to indoctrinate our children into supporting world government. Any and all other educational objectives must be sacrificed on the altar of this utopian dream.

Chapter Fifteen

Home Schools and Private Schools

Many of those involved in home schools and private schools believe that they are largely unaffected by the new federal education system of Goals 2000 and No Child Left Behind. They could not be more wrong.

Most private schools, for example, use the same textbooks as those used by public schools. This means that the Federal Curriculum themes of pantheism, postmodernism, new Marxism, radical multiculturalism, secular Humanism and world government are all aggressively promoted in many of the textbooks used by private schools. Private school teachers are theoretically supposed to be able to identify these hostile themes and deal with them appropriately. Is that actually happening? In most cases, no.

Private school teachers, as well as home school teachers, may become uncomfortable, however, with the extensive mythology and nature-worship now contained in their language arts books. They may also be concerned about the anti-American messages that are integrated into the history and civics books. We must keep in mind, however, that the radical federal agenda is effectively disguised. It operates under the cover of multiculturalism, environmentalism, global awareness and the like.

In addition, private school teachers are not trained to identify those truths that are missing from the educational materials. Even if the teachers can identify what is missing, it is the unusual private school teacher who has the time and background to supplement the textbooks being used. Chapter 16 explains those foundational principles of America that are usually either missing or redefined in the revisionist history and civics textbooks now used in our schools. Chapters 16, 19 and 20 describe in detail those principles that will play prominent roles in textbooks that are genuinely academic and are true to our history.

Part II of this book contains guidelines teachers can use to evaluate textbooks and other materials. The guidelines describe both the content that textbooks should contain as well as radical content that is best avoided. It is hoped that these guidelines will be useful both in textbook selection as well as in determining how to use various textbooks available.

The radical Federal Curriculum is also being aggressively marketed to private schools and home schools. The current McGraw-Hill *Home School Catalog: PreK-Grade 8*, for example, identifies one-third of its software and textbook offerings as being based on the national curriculum standards.

McGraw-Hill's new math textbook, for example, *Axel's Whirled Math Numbers and Equations* is described with the following language:

> Program concepts are based on **NCTM Standards** [integrated math] and many state curriculum frameworks. [p. 49]

The national curriculum standards which form the conceptual structure for the textbooks and software are always identified in bold print in this catalog to make sure the reader doesn't miss the point. The glossary for the catalog then draws on the conformity of its materials to the national standards as a way to promote its wares. The glossary states:

> **Standards**
> Statements regarding skills and concepts that should be accomplished on various levels of schooling. There are national as well as state standards that are to be met, and usually monitored through standardized testing. Many of our imprints meet National Standards set by national associations including NSTA, NCTM, NCTE and NCSS.

The implication of this definition for "standards" is that if parents want their children to do well on standardized tests, they should choose materials based on the national curriculum standards. This questionable implication and the prestige of the national standards are being used by the company to sell its products.

The catalog doesn't give parents and teachers the rest of the story, of course—that the national standards focus on teaching attitudes, values and behavior and are weak on teaching academic content. Students schooled in the national math standards, for example, will be inadequately prepared for college-level math because NCTM math is inferior for teaching math content (see Chapter 2).

Similarly, the 2004 McGraw-Hill mathematics catalog for public and private schools, called *Glencoe2004: Mathematics*, has an entire section on integrated (NCTM) math. In this section, the McGraw-Hill catalog states:

Research-Based and Classroom-Tested
Developed with funding from the **National Science Foundation,** each course in *Contemporary Mathematics in Context* is the product of a four-year research, development, and evaluation process involving thousands of students in schools across our country. [p. 34]

This glowing description of integrated math is technically accurate, but it is also highly misleading. The terms "research-based" and "classroom- tested," as noted earlier, are meaningless in today's world of education. The research and testing involved in integrated math were the result of $1 billion of our tax dollars spent by the National Science Foundation to develop and promote this flawed math program. Integrated math is really Marxist math (see Chapter 4), and is known to be defective.

In addition, the prestige of the National Science Foundation is used to promote this inferior product. The catalog doesn't say, of course, that the division of the National Science Foundation that is promoting NCTM math is dominated by the "like-minded" individuals described in Chapter 13. The agenda of these like-minded-with-UNESCO bureaucrats is political radicalism. Their agenda is not academic achievement. As a consequence of this misleading advertising, some home schools and private schools buy and use textbooks and other materials that are actually hostile to the goals of the schools.

There is also the matter of the new national achievement tests. Because these tests are now based on the Federal Curriculum, they no longer provide valid measurements of how much students are actually learning. Home-schooled children and children in private schools will probably continue to do reasonably well on the tests, but neither the parents nor the schools will know how well students are learning because the tests are no longer designed to primarily measure academic achievement.

The new SAT test is especially troubling. The revised SAT will include essay questions that are specifically designed to probe the attitudes, values, beliefs and worldview of the child. A SAT publication called "What Students will Ask about the new SAT—a Pocket Guide for Counselors," states:

Students will write an essay that requires them to take a position on an issue and use examples to support their position [p.2]...[And] the essay questions will ask you take a position on an issue and support it persuasively with examples from your studies and experiences. [p. 13]

The student's answer to these invasive questions will be part of the student's permanent record and will be accessible to any college, graduate school, or other institution which uses the SAT as an admission requirement. This means, first of all, that students are vulnerable to being scored higher or lower depending upon the degree of political correctness revealed in their answers. It also means that students may be subject to being admitted, or denied admission, to schools of higher learning, including medical schools and other graduate schools, on the basis of the attitudes, values and worldview they describe in answer to these probing questions.

Does this sound far-fetched? A recent "study" conducted by the National Science Foundation concluded that "social conservatives" are individuals who exhibit "mental rigidity" and "decreased cognitive function, lowered self-esteem, fear, anger, pessimism, disgust, and contempt." [http://www.educationnews.org/psychoanalyzingthepublic.htm] The implications for discrimination against social conservatives are obvious.

It must be recognized that the SAT questions described above are unprecedented in individual national achievement tests. Never before have the political and worldview positions of the child been considered fair game on required national tests. These new SAT tests demonstrate how totally corrupted our education system is becoming under the new centralized federal control. These abhorrent plans for the SAT are genuinely reminiscent of Joseph Stalin's Soviet Union. The reason for these new tests is that the SAT is part of an education system designed to transform the child, not educate the child. It is all part of the international system of education that intends to control the lives and minds of every person in the entire world. As observed earlier, the United States is the number-one target of the internationalists.

There are other significant features of the new SAT that will have a profound affect on private schools and home schools. In describing the new SAT, *Time* magazine of October 27, 2003, made this observation:

Girls tend to outperform boys on writing exams, so their overall scores could benefit from the addition of the new writing section. Boys usually score higher on the math section, but the new exam will contain fewer of the abstract-reasoning items at which they often excel.

These new features are consistent with the recommendations of Antonio Gramsci who said that education should favor the supposedly exploited classes (females) at the expense of the alleged ruling classes (males). *Time* also made this observation about the new SAT:

> At his [Board Chairman Gaston Caperton III] insistence, the goal of influencing school curriculum has become the overriding preoccupation of the new test's developers...But this is how powerful the test has become: many schools are already worrying about how to change their curriculums to fit the exam—even though the College Board has yet to finish a first draft of the first booklet. [Ibid.]

Is *Time* correct about this—that the primary purpose of the new SAT is dictating curriculum to our schools? We should not be surprised at this revelation. The SAT board chairman, Gaston Caperton III, is a close friend of Bill Clinton's former Education Secretary, Richard Riley, one of the architects of the federal education system. The primary goal of the federal education takeover has always been dictating the curriculum. That is what the national curriculum standards are all about.

Under No Child Left Behind, all states must write their own achievement tests based on their state standards. And what are the state standards based upon? The national curriculum standards, of course. The establishment of the Federal Curriculum is the primary focus of the new system. [See the author's book, *Fed Ed: The New Federal Curriculum: and How It's Enforced* (St. Paul: EdWatch, 2002).]

The federal education system is designed to be a seamless web that will catch all students and all schools. Goals 2000 repeatedly said that it covered "all students" and "all schools." The new SAT is specifically designed to pressure all schools, including home schools and private schools, to conform to the radical Federal Curriculum.

There are other problems with the new SAT. *Time* also said:

> As Lemann writes of the early rationale for the SAT, "Tests that require a student to write essays...are highly susceptible to the subjective judgments of the grader...so they have low reliability.... In June, I participated in a mock grading session with members of the College Board's writing-development committee. We read 15 essays by kids who had taken a pretest; they had been given 25 minutes to write on a topic I can't reveal, since it may appear on a future SAT. We scored the essays on a

scale of 1 to 6, 1 meaning 'very poor' organization and development and 6 meaning the student organized her thoughts, displayed 'facility' with language and 'insightfully addresses the writing task.' Such standards are quite rubbery, as we discovered: of the essays we read, we 25 readers uniformly agreed on a grade of none. On most of the essays, the lowest score was a 3 full points away from the highest." [*Time*, October 27, 2003]

Any test that lacks reliability puts kids from the best schools at a disadvantage. Keep in mind, however, that the new SAT is not intended to be a valid and reliable test of a student's ability or achievement. The new SAT is designed to drive the curriculum in the direction of the radical national curriculum standards.

Most, if not all, of the national tests are designed around the new federal education system—a system that is focused on promoting the agendas of the pantheists, postmodernists, new Marxists, secular Humanists and world federalists; the "like-minded" radicals who have succeeded in taking our education system hostage. For them education does not exist for academic accomplishment, nor does it exist for transmitting our American political system and culture. For those who are like-minded with UNESCO, education is the means by which they intend to create their brave new world, just as Antonio Gramsci said.

CHAPTER SIXTEEN

The Twelve Pillars
of Freedom

If we hope to be successful in returning our education system to one of academic excellence and one that respects the freedom and independence of the United states, we first must know what such a program looks like. Since civics and government provide the core curriculum of the new radical system, that is where we should begin our study.

The Declaration of Independence of the United States clarifies what it means to be a free nation; it needs to be taught and it needs to be taught accurately. It should be taught in both history and government classes. If our schools do begin to teach the Declaration accurately, we will have come a long way in having an education system that is academic, true to our history, and that clarifies what it means to be a free, sovereign nation.

The education radicals know this too. That is why teaching the Declaration of Independence accurately is a watershed, dividing academic, knowledge-based education and transformational education.

The Declaration of Independence clearly and emphatically promotes certain identifiable principles which have formed the foundation for government in the United States. John Quincy Adams gave recognition to these foundational principles when he said:

> The virtue which had been infused into the Constitution of the United States...was no other than...those abstract principles which had been first proclaimed in the Declaration of Independence—namely, the self-evident truths of the natural and unalienable rights of man...This was the platform upon which the Constitution of the United States had been erected.

Abraham Lincoln similarly made reference to the importance of these foundational principles when he said:

> I have never had a thought politically which did not spring from the sentiments embodied in the Declaration of Independence.

The Declaration contains 12 such sentiments, or principles. These 12 principles may properly be called, "The Twelve Pillars of Freedom." These principles are the following:

Pillar number 1: National Sovereignty. The Declaration of Independence begins by saying:

> When in the Course of human events it becomes necessary for one people to dissolve the political bands which have connected them with another, and to assume, among the Powers of the earth, the separate and equal station to which the Laws of Nature and Nature's God entitle them, a decent respect to the opinions of mankind requires they should declare the causes which impel them to the separation.

This grand declaration that "one people" will now "assume among the Powers of the earth the separate and equal station" is a bold and clear statement of national sovereignty. The Declaration of Independence begins with national sovereignty. It also ends with national sovereignty. Indeed, the Declaration of Independence could just as well be called the "Declaration of National Sovereignty" because that is what the Declaration means.

National sovereignty is the primary battle-ground in the war over academic education versus international education as specified by the new Federal Curriculum. The primary goal of the internationalists is disbanding the national sovereignty of the United States.

As we observed in Chapter 14, the one textbook authorized and funded as part of the federal education system never mentions national sovereignty; it is out of sight and out of mind. In evaluating state education standards and textbooks in American history and government, therefore, the first item to look for is national sovereignty. The reader will find that most state education standards and many history and government textbooks never mention national sovereignty. National sovereignty is intended to be out of sight and out of mind. That is how successful the radicals have been in rewriting the history and civics curriculum of the United States. In evaluating textbooks and state standards, compare the number of times the term "national sovereignty" is used to the number of times "global" or "United Nations" is used. That comparison will tell the story of what is being taught.

Pillar number 2: Natural Law. Our Declaration of Independence says that the United States became an independent nation based on the "Laws of Nature and Nature's God" as stated above. That is, our nation is based on natural law. What is "natural law"? It is the universal moral code that governs all people. Its precepts include equality, justice, the Golden Rule, the recognition that human beings have more value than plants, animals and objects, and the inalienable human rights of life, liberty and property.

Natural law directly confronts the allegation that morality is primarily a matter of individual choice or a construct of culture. Natural law asserts that morality is universal and is to be recognized and followed by all people and all cultures. Natural law, for example, asserts that murder is wrong, slavery is wrong, theft is wrong, slander is wrong, etc. regardless of the culture one lives in. Natural law forms the basis of any legitimate appeal to "crimes against humanity" as utilized in international law.

Natural law also forms the basis for inalienable rights. Why, for example, is murder wrong? It is because of the natural law principle that people have a right to life. That is, the right to life is part of the universal moral code we know as natural law. The role of governments, then, is to write its law based on natural law which protects the inalienable right to life. Our forefathers understood this principle, and that is why they often said that "law is discovered, not made."

A college-level American government textbook, American Government: Roots and Reform, (1993 Edition) provides a good description of natural law as it states:

> **Where Did Our Ideas of Government Come From?** ...classical and medieval writers such as St. Thomas Aquinas (1225-1274) argued that...governments were ordained by natural law—basic and God-given rules that do not have to be written as much as discovered. Individual rights to life and liberty were a part of the natural law created by God. [Karen O'Connor and Larry J. Sabato (New York: Longman Publishing, 1993), p. 6]

As correctly described by this textbook, our nation's founders saw natural law as being the universal standard of right and wrong which is part of the world God created. Natural law is understood as having been created by the person the Declaration calls "the Supreme Judge of the world." That is, natural law is defined as being God-given and being God's law; it is not the confused "man is his natural state" concept of natural law which can mean almost anything.

Most state standards, as well as textbooks, either omit or minimize natural law—the reason being that they wish to eliminate the foundation of our national sovereignty as well as eliminating the basis for our inalienable rights.

Pillar number 3: Self-evident truths. The Declaration states:

We hold these truths to be self-evident....

As noted above, the proposed Minnesota education standards advocated by the Democrat-controlled Senate made no reference whatsoever to "self-evident truths." These same standards did, however, use the words "change" or "changing" 24 times. (The House position which included "self-evident truths" prevailed in conference committee.) As we have seen in earlier chapters, postmodernists and the new Marxists believe there is no such thing as truth. They assert that all knowledge consists of "constructs"—mental images created by the powerful to exploit the vulnerable. As we saw in Chapter 2, the reason that integrated math is such a disaster is because it is based on the postmodernist/Marxist worldview which asserts that math is a mere construct, not a matter of reality.

As we observed in earlier chapters, the entire Federal Curriculum has been written on the assumptions of postmodernism and new Marxism. That is why history is "deconstructed" and why students must "construct" their own views of knowledge.

The federal education system embraces the postmodernist view of education because the radicals want to eliminate the Twelve Pillars of Freedom of the United States. The radicals want students to believe that the principles of freedom, as stated in the Declaration of Independence, may have been acceptable for the people of America of that time, but they are not necessarily true for us today. Worse yet, the education change-agents often argue that our nation's foundational principles are really constructs used by the powerful to exploit everyone else. Either way, the radicals want to eliminate all the principles that have made our country a free and independent nation.

Pillar number 4: Equality. The Declaration of Independence says:

We hold these truths to be self-evident, that all men are created equal....

110

The federal education system does not actually eliminate the word "equal," but it falsely defines what "equal" means. That is, the federal education system treats "equal" or "equality" as though it means treating everyone the same. The brilliant Harvard psychologist and researcher, Lawrence Kohlberg, however, correctly explained that equality does not mean treating everyone the same. Equality, said Kohlberg, means treating everyone's legitimate claims the same. For example, one person has a legitimate claim to a piece of property, another person does not. Equality does not mean treating two people the same as far as that property is concerned. One person has a legitimate claim as a parent of a child; another person has no such claim. Equality, regarding the supervision of that child, means treating the person who has a legitimate claim as parent quite differently from others who do not have that legitimate claim.

In contrast to the examples above, everyone has a legitimate claim to freedom—that is why slavery is wrong. Everyone has a legitimate claim to own property—that is why theft is wrong. Everyone has a legitimate claim to life—that is why murder and abortion are wrong. Everyone has a legitimate claim to self-defense—that is why our Constitution guarantees the right to own and bear arms.

One of the most obvious applications of the false definition of equality used by the education radicals is their promotion of the gay rights agenda, an integral feature of the Federal Curriculum. If equality means treating everyone the same, then marriage should be altered to accommodate homosexuals. If, on the other hand, equality is accurately defined, then the real question is whether homosexuals have a legitimate claim to redefine marriage—which they do not. The fact that most members of the American public oppose homosexual marriage may be explained in part by their intuitive sense of what equality actually means as well as their sense of what constitutes marriage.

Pillar number 5: Inalienable Rights. The Declaration of Independence states:

> We hold these truths to be self-evident, that all men are created equal, that they are endowed by their Creator with certain unalienable Rights....

Our forefathers understood that since our rights have been given to us by God, these rights are "unalienable." Today we say "inalienable." Our forefathers recognized that the fundamental human rights, such as life, liberty and property, are not granted by government; they have been granted by God. The role of government, then, is to protect these God-given rights. The founders of our nation defined our government in such a way as to clarify that government had a lower level of authority than the inalienable rights of its people. Rights do not depend on government; government rests on the human rights. The Ninth and Tenth Amendments to our constitution clarify this all-important principle.

Totalitarian governments, such as communist governments, see it the other way around. The constitution of Cuba, for example, says:

> Citizens have freedom of speech in keeping with the goals of the socialist society.

In other words, in Cuba the decisions of the government have higher standing than any human rights people may have. Totalitarian governments do not deny that people have basic rights; they do deny, however, that these rights are "inalienable." They deny that human rights have a higher ranking than government policies.

The UN Universal Declaration of Human Rights, 1948, has often been described as an attempt to find a compromise between the view that human rights are inalienable and the Communist view that rights are subject to government policies. This UN document accomplishes this attempted compromise by saying that rights are "inalienable" in its Preamble, but after the Preamble, in that part of the document where rights are explained, the UN document always describes rights merely as "rights." We can't have it both ways. Either rights are inalienable or they are not. The UN Universal Declaration of Human Rights clarifies the inconsistency at the end of the document when it states:

> These rights and freedoms may in no case be exercised contrary to the purposes and principles of the United Nations.

This UN document means that its government policies have a higher value than human rights. For that reason, human rights are not treated as being genuinely inalienable. For that reason, the view of human rights contained in the UN Declaration of Human Rights is essentially the Communist view of rights. It is not the American view of inalienable rights.

The new Federal Curriculum consistently advocates the totalitarian view of human rights contained in the UN Declaration of Human Rights. The reader is advised to read through the state education standards and the textbooks being used in his state. The reader will probably find that the radical UN view of rights, not the American view, is being taught.

Pillar number 6: The inalienable Right to Life. The Declaration of Independence states:

> ...they are endowed by their Creator with certain unalienable Rights, that among these are Life, Liberty, and the pursuit of Happiness....

The education radicals do not want to admit to the inalienable right to life because this right interferes with their agendas of abortion on-demand, euthanasia, and their desire to substantially reduce the population of the world. The new education system will speak of the right to life, however, but this right is not treated as an inalienable right. Other government objectives, therefore, such as 'freedom of choice," will be given priority over the right to life.

It is unfortunate that pro-life groups, such as National Right to Life, have yet to understand that the right to life which they exist to protect is being undermined by the new Federal Curriculum. These groups must come to understand that they are "giving away the store" by not being involved in the battle for America in our schools, which is also the battle for the right to life.

Pillar number 7: The Inalienable Right to Liberty. The new Federal Curriculum speaks of liberty as a right, but, once again, liberty is not viewed as an inalienable right. The federal education system is also engaged in misleading the public about what freedom means by redefining fundamental terms that relate to liberty. These terms are:

A. **Republic.** The United States Constitution guarantees a "republican" form of government. By that term is meant a *representative form of government* where voters elect government officials who will carry out the necessary governmental functions. That is what "republic" or "republican" means. The Federal Curriculum standards, in contrast, define "republican" to mean that form of government which believes that *the common good is more important than individual rights*. "Common good" is always defined by government, of course. The net effect of this definition shift is that "republic" is defined by the federal education system to mean the UN view of human rights which is the same as the Communist view of rights defined above. *As a consequence, the public is led to believe that the word "republican" is being used to represent freedom, when it has actually been redefined to mean the opposite.*

A. **Democracy.** By common usage, "democracy" has come to mean the same as "republic"—having a *representative form of government*. Once again, however, the education radicals have redefined the term. "Democracy" in the new Federal Curriculum does not mean representative government where each citizen has one vote. Not at all. By "democracy" the education radicals mean *power-sharing among various groups*. Among the groups that share the power are non-governmental organizations (NGOs), such as the Center for Civic Education, consisting of people who never face voters in any way. NGOs are totally self-appointed. The term "civil society" is used in the new system to refer to these NGOs. At the UN, the leadership decides which NGOs it wishes to recognize and which ones it will ignore. *As a consequence, the word "democracy" in the new federal system actually means totalitarianism—absolute rule by those on the top who claim that what they are doing is democratic when it is actually the exact opposite.*

Pillar number 8: The Inalienable Right to Private Property. The Declaration of Independence uses the term "pursuit of happiness" for this right. Amendments 5 and 14 to the United States Constitution state that no person may be deprived of his/her "life, liberty, or property" without due process of law. That is, the Constitution clarifies that "pursuit of happiness" refers primarily to the right of personal property.

The new education system speaks of the right of personal property, but it, once again, does not speak of this right as inalienable. Similarly, it over-emphasizes and exaggerates various global environmental issues while at the same time minimizing property rights. The notion of the global commons is emphasized. The "global commons" refers to those features of the globe which are supposedly owned by all people in common—the oceans, all the water resources of the world including all watersheds, the air including the atmosphere over every country, and all the natural resources including the fish in the sea, all oil and petroleum and all minerals. The UN, the argument goes, must manage the global commons—the global resources—on behalf of all global citizens.

Because the Federal Curriculum does not respect the inalienable right of private property, it generally avoids the terms "free market" and "free enterprise." It will instead use the term "market economy" which can mean almost anything including socialism and the third-way economics described by Anthony Giddens.

This fault-line, also, was part of the battle in Minnesota over rewriting the state's education standards. The Democrat-controlled Senate removed the term "free market" from the standards proposed by the citizens' committee. The reason Democrats avoid the words "free market" is because "free market" implies private ownership of property and decision-making by the private sector. This was an area where the citizens' committee in Minnesota prevailed. As a consequence, Minnesota may now be the only state in the union which specifies that our economic system is a primarily a free market system.

The world government crowd, in contrast, wants government involved in the making of economic decisions and wants governments to be able to own or share ownership in businesses. Global government advocates also call for the unholy marriage of government, education and business—a union formed in the United States through School-to-Work. STW unapologetically symbolizes this union by the three intersecting circles in its logo.

Pillar number 9: The primary purpose of government is the protection of the inalienable rights. The Declaration of Independence states it this way:

> That, to secure these Rights, Governments are instituted among Men....

According to the Declaration, government has one over-arching purpose—protecting the inalienable rights of all people. The new Federal Curriculum distorts this pillar of freedom and says instead that government has two purposes—protecting human rights and promoting the common good. Because "the common good" will always be defined by government, the protection of human rights can always be overruled by government policy, just as the UN Declaration of Human Rights asserts is the case.

Pillar number 10: Popular Sovereignty. The Declaration of Independence states this pillar with the words:

> That to secure these Rights, Governments are instituted among Men, deriving their just powers from the consent of the governed.

The Declaration clarifies that people have a higher level of authority than government, and government has only those powers delegated to it by the citizens. Following the principles of the Declaration, the Constitution of the United States was created to be a social contract by which the states and the people designated some of their powers to the federal government for the sake of good order and national defense.

The entire federal education system is a violation of this principle of popular sovereignty. Under our Constitution, education policy is a power reserved for the states and the people. Neither the states nor the people have changed that principle so as to give the federal government any authority whatsoever in the field of education. Keep in mind also the new, and radical, definitions of "republic" and "democracy" as explained above. In view of these new definitions, "popular sovereignty" to the revisionists no longer means genuine democracy or being a genuine republic. At best, "popular sovereignty" to the transformational education crowd means the post-democratic system of the European Union where the top government officials are all appointed—they never face the voters.

Pillar number 11: Federalism and States' Rights. The last paragraph of the Declaration of Independence says:

> That these United States are, and of Right ought to be, free and independent states; that they are Absolved from all Allegiance to the British Crown, and that all political connection between them and the State of Great Britain is, and ought to be totally dissolved; and that as Free and Independent States, they have full Power to levy War, conclude Peace, contract Alliances, establish Commerce and do all other Acts and Things which Independent States may of right do.

In this way the Declaration of Independence emphatically affirmed the sovereignty of the federal United States and the sovereignty of the separate states. This Declaration envisioned a federal system of government with the states delegating some of their power to the federal government while retaining other powers, such as education, for themselves.

The federal system of government is explained in the Tenth Amendment to the Constitution which stipulates that any powers not specifically delegated to the federal government by the Constitution are reserved for the states and the people respectively. It should not be surprising, then, that the Federal Curriculum minimizes or ignores the Tenth Amendment. As explained in Chapter 14, it is not possible to teach the doctrine of limited government without teaching the Tenth Amendment. That is the intent. The education radicals do not believe in limited government; they do not want it taught. The brave new world they envision will control all the people of the earth. Neither the people, nor the states, nor the national governments will have an adequate check on that absolute power.

This observation is especially significant in view of the fact that the world government crowd uses the formation of the United States as a model for the formation of world government. They say that just as the several states in the United States came together over 200 years ago to form a centralized federal government, so also the time has come for the nations of the world to come together and form a world federation. Since these world federalists recognize no reserved powers for the states in the United States, we have every reason to believe that they will similarly recognize no reserved powers for the nations after their world federation is formed.

Pillar number 12: Divine Providence. The Declaration of Independence ends with this sentence:

> And for the support of this Declaration, with a firm reliance on the Protection of Divine Providence, we mutually pledge to each other our Lives, our Fortunes and our sacred Honor.

The colonists stated their conviction that there is a God in the Heavens who ultimately governs in the affairs of men. The signers of the Declaration were convinced that their cause was just and that the just God, earlier in the Declaration referred to as the "Supreme Judge of the world," would be on their side. This statement of belief is totally consistent with the pillars of freedom stated earlier. There is no Natural Law without a Law-giver. The unalienable rights, they said, were God-given. Equality, they said, was the state in which we were created by God. If there is no creator God, there is no reason to affirm the equality of all people, nor is there any reason to believe that people have any inherent rights.

The new Federal Curriculum, in contrast, has no time for divine providence. The new Masters see themselves as the final decision-makers of what is right and true and good for the whole. They have taken upon themselves the obligation of creating the utopian dream of the one world: one-world religion, one-world culture, one-world education system with one-world curriculum, and one-world government under their control.

Chapter Seventeen

Winning the
Battle for America

The Twelve Pillars of Freedom form the philosophical/ religious foundation of the United States of America. These Pillars are the reason we are a free people living in a free nation. They are largely the reason that our nation is the world's only superpower. They are the reason that the United States is the beacon-light of freedom throughout the world. These twelve principles did in fact usher in "morning in America," a truth recognized and appreciated by most Americans.

These Twelve Pillars of Freedom explain why students in China's Tiananmen Square held copies of our Declaration of Independence in their hands. They did so because they, too, wanted to be free. They wanted China to recognize their inherent freedom just like the United States does. They wanted to have the same freedom that the internationalists are now so eager to take away from us.

As we evaluate state standards, national standards and school textbooks, the Twelve Pillars of Freedom will serve as our guide. These principles describe the central tenets of our true history. They describe the foundation of our system of government. They also form the basis of what public education in our nation is meant to be.

When we revise our state education standards, and as we demand better textbooks, these Twelve Pillars of Freedom must form the philosophical foundation of what we are willing to accept. Wisdom of the past does exist. Truth does exist. This truth can be known and communicated. This truth can be taught to our children. There is such a thing as real history; history that can be known; history that can be taught; history that can be tested; history that attests to those truths that have stood the ultimate test of time.

Our forefathers pledged their lives and their fortunes in defense of these Pillars of Freedom. Millions of brave Americans have risked and given their all in defense of these same principles. The question for us now is: Are we willing to carry on the American dream by being willing to fight for these principles too?

We can win the battle for America. We can win this battle for freedom the same way the War for Independence was won; by first communicating to our fellow Americans the truth about what is happening. Truth always precedes freedom. People will choose freedom only when they first know what is true. People are armed to fight for freedom only when they know the truth.

This book is designed to be a first step in winning back our freedom. Everything in this book is accurate. It is based on the important documents themselves and on what the other side has said. The reader is invited to scrutinize every word. The observations are not exaggerated. They are not taken out of context. This book is merely a report on what is happening to our country. This book tells it like it is. It tells the story the media refuses to tell.

We citizens have no one to blame but ourselves. We have sat back and allowed what is described in this book to happen to us. True, our state and national leaders have failed us, but in a free nation, remaining free is ultimately up to us.

The future of our children, the future of our nation, is in our hands. Don't ask someone else to fight the fight for freedom on your behalf. If that is your response—to let someone else sacrifice for your freedom—then ask yourself if you deserve to be free. Our forefathers over many generations have given us our legacy of freedom. They were willing to make the sacrifices necessary, to do whatever was necessary. Are we going to be the generation that gives it all away?

This is what we need to do: We first need to inform other Americans about what is happening. This book is written for that purpose. It is designed to be easy to read. Make use of it. Order additional copies. Do whatever it takes to get the truth out to more Americans.

We secondly need to form a national organization or network that can represent us in Washington and hopefully in every state government as well. Individually we can do nothing, but organized into a national network, we can win this war. We are making real progress in Minnesota. We were the first state in the union to throw out the radical Federal Curriculum. This step, however, is just the beginning. We now need to turn the corner in Washington D. C. and in every other state in our nation as well.

Thirdly we need to inform our elected officials. Very few of them know what is happening. Those who do know are mostly the advocates of global government. The architects of the radical federal and international system of education have no intention of telling our lawmakers the truth. Many of the change-agents are inside the federal and state bureaucracies. Some of them are elected officials. All of them know that if the public and lawmakers learn what is really happening, the patriots will win.

Lawmakers have been given false information about the federal education system for years. It will not be easy to convince them of the truth. At the same time, truth is naturally more persuasive than falsehood. That is the basic premise of freedom of speech. The information really does speak for itself.

Let the battle begin. Up to this point, the other side has been like a team on a football field with no organized opposition (that focuses on education policy). The education internationalists have run up and down the field scoring points with little opposition. It is not surprising they have been so successful. No organization which specializes in education policy has existed to oppose them.

The time has come to change that. In doing so, we must remember that our forefathers put their trust in the Supreme Judge of the universe. We must do the same. It is a David versus Goliath type of battle, but let us never forget that it was David who won. Why did David succeed? He did so for two reasons: He trusted in the King of Kings, and he was willing to fight. Do we wish that anything more could be said of us?

This is the battle for America. It is the battle of our time. It is being fought in our schools. It needs to be fought in Congress. It needs to be fought in every state of the union. The battle is ours—to win or to lose.

Following are some of the changes we need to make:

At the Federal Level

1. Federal lawmakers and American citizens need to be informed about the information contained in this book. Truth always precedes freedom. The citizens of our nation must bring this information to the rest of our people and our lawmakers. See also the web page www.edwatch.org which describes other materials including videos, CDs, tapes, essays and additional materials that are useful for this task. Sign up to be on EdWatch's e-mail update list.

2. We need to form a national organization for promoting good education policy. Stay tuned to www.edwatch.org and the e-mail update list for information.

3. The national organization must lobby elected officials at the federal level. The goal of lobbying is bringing accurate information to lawmakers as well as making specific recommendations for change.

4. The Department of Education should be prohibited from establishing and promoting national standards (Federal Curriculum). Congress has passed legislation attempting to do just that (NCLB Sec. 9527 b). What Congress doesn't know is that federal bureaucrats and those employing insider politics have done an end-run around the law.

5. No Child Left Behind should be repealed. (See Chapters 10, 11 and 12.) Schools should instead be encouraged to abandon progressive education and adopt those strategies that actually work in raising the academic achievement of all students.

6. The federal government's NAEP test must be available for public scrutiny. The radical agenda of the test would then be exposed and corrected. Each year, the test questions should be made public in a reasonable period of time after it is administered. State participation in the NAEP should also be strictly voluntary as it was prior to 2002.

7. In order to remain faithful to our Constitution, any education initiatives on the part of the federal government must be genuinely voluntary. This means that state participation in federal education programs should not be tied to federal funding. It also means that participation in one program should not be linked to funding for other programs.

8. Congress should reaffirm the Twelve Pillars of Freedom and encourage all schools to teach them.

AT STATE AND LOCAL LEVELS

1. State lawmakers and citizens need to be informed about the information contained in this book. Citizens in each state must bring this information to its lawmakers and to the rest of its population. See the web page www.edwatch.org which describes other materials including videos, CDs, tapes, essays and other materials that are useful for this task. Sign up to be on EdWatch's e-mail update list.

2. Each state needs to form a state organization. Each state organization needs to establish its own website and its own e-mail update list.

3. States organizations must lobby their elected officials. The goal of lobbying is bringing accurate information to lawmakers as well as making specific recommendations for positive changes in state laws and policies.

4. All education standards at the state level, local level or both, need to be rewritten. All state and national achievement tests

also need to be rewritten. (NCLB requires states to base their achievement tests on their state standards which are now mostly based on the radical Federal Curriculum.)

5. All education standards and tests should be consistent with the Twelve Pillars of Freedom and be genuinely academic in nature. Part II of this book gives guidelines for writing such standards and tests.

6. States must revise their teacher certification requirements so they conform to the principles of knowledge-based education.

7. Textbook selection, whether done at the state level or local level, should use as guidelines the Twelve Pillars of Freedom as well as other information and guidelines supplied in this book.

8. Citizens involved in home schools and private schools need to become better informed about the new federal education system and its huge impact on their schools. Decisions need to made accordingly.

9. Americans who believe in the Twelve Pillars of Freedom and the importance of knowledge-based education should run for public office including that of local school board and all elected offices at the state and national levels.

10. Coalitions need to be created with other organizations that are also committed to some or all of the Twelve Pillars of Freedom.

11. Local schools should avoid the International Baccalaureate and the GLOBE Program (see Appendix B and H).

Part II

Guidelines for State Standards, Tests, Textbooks and Curricula

Chapter Eighteen

The Importance of Changing State Education Standards

The federal education law, No Child Left Behind (NCLB), requires each state to have state education standards. NCLB says:

> Each state plan shall demonstrate that the state has developed challenging academic content standards and challenging student academic achievement standards that will be used by the state, its local educational agencies, and its schools. [Title I, Part A, Subpart 1, Sec. 1111(b)(1)(A)]

As can be seen from the section of law quoted above, states are required to specify the "content standards," (curriculum) that all state schools must teach, and also specify minimum "achievement standards" (proficiency levels) that all students in state schools must accomplish to make satisfactory progress.

NCLB also requires:

> Each state plan shall demonstrate that the state has implemented academic assessments ..." [And] "Such assessments shall be aligned with the state's challenging academic content and student academic achievement standards....[Title I, Part A, Subpart 1, Sec. 1111(b)(3)]

NCLB requires states to base their achievement tests on their state standards. Since schools will teach to the test, NCLB has the effect of essentially requiring all public schools to organize their curriculum around the state standards since that is what their students will be tested on. Keep in mind that NCLB requires states to test their students each year in reading and math in grades 3-8 and at least once in grades 9-12. The results of these tests determine if schools are meeting Adequate Yearly Progress (AYP) or if they are on the road to becoming failed schools, a status that brings with it substantial penalties. As was described in Part I of this book, the state standards for all 50 states are largely based on the national standards (Federal Curriculum).

For all these reasons, reforming our state education standards is absolutely critical if we wish to have academic programs that are knowledge-based and pro-American. Minnesota is the first state to have begun this reform. (Alabama has also begun the process.) In the spring of 2003 Minnesota threw out its Goals 2000-based state standards. These standards were modeled after the Federal Curriculum. In 2003 Minnesota adopted new reading and math standards. In the spring of 2004 Minnesota adopted new science and social studies standards.

NCLB does not directly require schools to test students in the social studies areas, but the new Federal Curriculum specifies that social studies will be incorporated into all other subject areas. This is especially true in language arts (reading). For this reason, the social studies standards will largely determine the content of the literature being used as well as the content of history, geography, psychology, civics and government. The social studies curriculum will also play a prominent role in science classes.

One of the difficulties citizens face is that most legislators are unaware of the content of their state education standards. Many legislators have no idea that these standards even exist. Citizens will find it necessary to access their state education standards, see what those standards say, and show their legislators what their standards are and what they mean. (Citizens in some states will need to work directly with their state boards of education.)

For example, Minnesota's education standards, prior to the spring of 2003, said:

> The Minnesota People and Cultures Framework refers primarily to the social science content as described in the National Standards for Civics and Government (NSCG), National Geography Standards: 1994 (NGS), and National Standards for United States History (NSUSH).

Many state education standards will contain statements like the one above. Such statements clarify that the state education standards are based on the national standards. In order for citizens to deal with the perceived prestige of the national standards, it will be necessary to understand that the national standards are genuinely radical in their requirements. None of the 50 states contain a majority of citizens who will support the content of the national standards if they only know what those standards say. (See the author's book, *Fed Ed: The New Federal Curriculum and How It's Enforced*, available at Amazon.com or edwatch.org.)

Minnesota's pre-2003 state social studies standards said:

> Social studies is the disciplined inquiry or study of people who (all) live at the intersection of nature and culture (human-made environments). This human/environmental interaction defines needs which are satisfied through the construction of institutions, all of which serve to meet the needs created by specific cultures and special earth locations. For example, political institutions are constructed to keep order and to allocate power, resources and values.

What is wrong with this statement? Part I of this book explained that the words "construction" and "constructed" have a clear meaning in education today. Any form of the word "construct" means that knowledge and institutions are mere creations of a particular culture. This is the language of postmodernism and the new Marxism—the worldviews which say that we must "deconstruct" our country, its basic institutions and knowledge itself and "reconstruct" them as something different.

The questions that must be asked include: Is there such a thing as truth? If so, the standards must say so. Does real history exist—history that is knowable, teachable and testable? If so, the standards must say so. Are there genuine principles of good government—principles such as inalienable rights and national sovereignty? If so, the standards must say so. Does marriage have universal characteristics or is it merely a creation of culture? Marriage does have universal characteristics and state standards should treat the institution of marriage that way.

Minnesota's pre-2003 state geography standards said:

> [Students know] how to locate regions of the United States and selected regions of the world and identify geographic features and cultural characteristics of regions.

Citizens need to look closely at what standards don't say as well as at what they do say. State standards typically organize geography around regions and then ignore the major nations, their capitals and the 50 states of the United States and their capitals. Minnesota's pre-2003 geography standards, for example, did not require that students know the locations of any of the nations of the world except the United States. The education radicals want to eliminate nations; that is why they are ignored. Good geography standards will require that students know all 50 states and their capitals, all the major nations of the world, the oceans, major rivers and seas. Radical standards also focus too much on reading maps and forming "mental maps" as opposed to requiring that students actually know the locations of major nations, cities, mountain ranges and the like.

Minnesota's pre-2003 economics standards said:

> Through the use of fundamental concepts of economics, a student shall demonstrate understanding of the interactive nature of global, national, and local economic systems....

The problem, once again, is in what the education standards do not say. Minnesota's economics standards, for example, used the term "global" on numerous occasions, but never used the terms "free-enterprise" or "free-market." For that reason Minnesota citizens insisted, and succeeded, in convincing the legislature to specify that students must learn that the U. S. economy is primarily a free-market system. They must also now understand free-enterprise. References to "global" and "globalism" were substantially reduced.

The examples above provide a small sample of the issues citizens face in revising their state education standards. It is the experience of EdWatch that the issues are basically the same in all states. The remainder of Part II of this book will provide guidelines for revising state standards. The same guidelines can be used to evaluate textbooks and curricula.

CHAPTER NINETEEN

Criteria for History and Geography

The following guidelines can be used to evaluate textbooks, other books, tests, school curricula, school objectives, state education standards and national education standards. The guidelines distinguish between transformational education and academic education.

Transformational education includes the promotion of pantheism/New Age religion, multiculturalism including postmodernism and new Marxism, and world government. Transformational education is designed to undermine the principles and values which under gird the independence and sovereignty of the United States. Since Western culture is largely based on Christianity, transformational education is also intended to undermine Christianity. Transformational education is designed to change the student's values, attitudes and beliefs as opposed to providing an education that is primarily academic in nature.

Academic education, in contrast, emphasizes the teaching of information and skills. Academic education believes that critical thinking is important, but also believes that critical thinking is primarily based on knowledge. Academic education is knowledge-based. In the United States academic education also teaches the fundamental principles which form the basis of our U.S. government. Academic education in the United States recognizes Western exceptionalism and American exceptionalism.

Curriculum Guidelines for History and Geography
Transformational Education versus Academic Education

1. The Purpose of Education

Transformational Education: Believes that the purpose of education is to make radical changes in the nature of our people, government, basic institutions, all of society and our entire world. Defines the purpose of education in terms of changing the attitudes, values and worldview of learners. Trains children to be political activists.

Academic Education: Believes that the purpose of education is the transmission of academic knowledge and skills to the next generation. This traditional view reflects confidence in our form of government and in our other basic institutions and believes that even though our government and other institutions may be modified, their basic structures should also be preserved.

2. Models of History

Transformational Education: Rejects the Western heritage model of history and instead assumes that all cultures are equal. As a consequence it covers three or more cultures equally. No more than 33 per cent of world history material deals with the West. Adopts the "Convergence of Cultures Model" of world history. American history is organized around the same theme ("three cultures meet"). This theme is based on the worldview of multiculturalism. Non-Western cultures are pictured in a positive light overall, while Western cultures are pictured in a negative light. Emphasizes the reading of mythology and often treats mythology as being "oral history." Emphasizes various "perspectives" on history as opposed to "knowledge" of history.

Academic Education: Adopts the "Western Heritage Model" of history because the West (Europe and the United States) has played the leadership role, especially in the last 500 years or so, in science, medicine, economics, agriculture, the arts, high technology, religion, and government. Charles Murray, for example, described the results of his recent research by saying:

> I was surprised by the degree of concentration of accomplishment in Europe from 1400 to 1950 (the cutoff date for my data). This is not to say that the great civilizations of Greece, China, India and the Arab world did not do great things, but the ocean of accomplishment in Europe from 1400 to 1950 is truly staggering. I was also surprised to find how important religion was in the story of human accomplishment. [*World* magazine, 1-10-03, p. 26.]

The traditional view of history is less about culture, including mythology, than about historical information. It emphasizes written records and is skeptical about the accuracy of oral traditions.

3. Social Marxism versus American Exceptionalism

Transformational Education: Divides all cultures and other groups into two categories—oppressor groups and oppressed groups. Believes that the primary reason some groups or nations have lower standards of living than other groups is because the weaker groups have been exploited by the powerful groups. Evaluates countries, racial groups and other groups on the basis of disparities, not in terms of absolute achievements. The goal of various policies becomes the elimination of disparities, not the improvement of all groups. Supports income redistribution between nations and giving away technology to poor nations to eliminate these disparities. Education becomes more focused on reducing disparities than on "lifting all ships." Diversity training in an example of this theme.

Academic Education: Promotes the view that the reason the West, and especially the United States, has been successful is due to the foundational principles of these nations and to various characteristics of their cultures. (See Chapter 16.) Believes that success or failure is more the result of following certain definable principles than in exploiting others or being exploited by others. Argues that other nations can be successful by adopting those principles and characteristics which have proven to be related to success. Is more interested in raising the achievement of all nations, and all students, than in eliminating disparities. Believes that "a rising tide raises all ships."

4. Postmodernism versus Real Knowledge

Transformational Education: Views academic disciplines as consisting of constructs, not knowledge. History becomes a study of what various groups think about history ("multiple perspectives"). Students are expected to form their own conclusions—to construct historical knowledge based on their own investigations. "Constructs" are the interpretations of various cultures; they are not the same as truth or reality. Constructs are seen as being formed by powerful cultures, or powerful people in those cultures, to keep the vulnerable under control. Real history is viewed as nonexistent because history is seen as the interpretation of the powerful used to keep themselves in power. History is constructed, not discovered. "Knowledge" is matter of consensus. This education philosophy is known as radical constructivism, postmodernism and social Marxism.

Academic Education: Believes that intellectual disciplines such as history contain real knowledge even though no historian is totally objective.

Believes that history is knowable, teachable and testable. Acknowledges the existence of universal principles regarding science, mathematics, human behavior, economics, etc. Sees these principles as being knowable. Says that these universal principles are in operation whether they are recognized or not–an example being free-market economics. Emphasizes the transmission of knowledge as being the primary function of education. Agrees that much of education involves constructs but also believes that genuine information and truth exist. Argues that it is possible to distinguish between constructs versus information, facts and truth.

5. Internationalism versus Nationalism

Transformational Education: Emphasizes regions, cultures and various people-groups, as opposed to nations. Global organizations and treaties are highlighted. The Universal Declaration of Human Rights is portrayed as superior to the U.S. Bill of Rights. "Democracy" is redefined in globalist terms to mean power sharing among chosen groups and/or appointed office holders as opposed to rule by the people. Supports the continued expansion of the United Nations and its agencies to include, as examples, the International Criminal Court, an international system of education, the new UN standing police force and agreements which bring about increased international control of the environment such as the Kyoto Treaty and the Treaty on Biodiversity. Says that government has two primary purposes, not just one—protecting human rights and promoting the common good.

Academic Education: Emphasizes the role of nations in the world stage. Protecting inherent rights, controlling pollution, controlling crime, conducting education programs and the like are pictured as being the responsibilities of national governments, not international organizations. The Universal Declaration of Human Rights is viewed as being inferior to the U.S. Bill of Rights because the Bill of Rights acknowledges that basic human rights are inherent and are to be protected by government while the Universal Declaration of Human Rights sees human rights as being subordinate to the policies of the United Nations. Holds that government has one primary purpose—protecting our inalienable rights. Recognizes that the formation of a world government will lead to the elimination of our national sovereignty and personal freedom.

6. Relative Morality versus Universal Moral Principles

Transformational Education: Humanism and modern liberalism hold that morality is relative to the individual. The new education system believes that morality is relative to the culture (postmodernism and Antonio Gramsci). Marriage, for example, is viewed as a construct of the culture and can, therefore, be redefined to include gay marriage. Nontraditional roles for women are over-emphasized. Human rights such as life, liberty and property are seen as constructs that can be redefined. History and various institutions are viewed as needing to be "deconstructed" and "reconstructed." Modesty is defined as being a social construct used to keep the vulnerable under control. Obscenity is used for the purpose of undermining modesty. The elitists see their role as being change-agents for the deconstruction and reconstruction of society. Human rights are described as "basic," but not as "unalienable," "inherent" or "God-given."

Academic Education: Sees moral values as universal and as needing to be recognized and followed, not created (natural law). Recognizes that universal moral values include the golden rule, justice, equality, the right to life, the right to own personal property, the right of liberty, freedom of speech, freedom of religion, and the right of self-protection. Recognizes that these moral values are discovered, not made. Believes that these moral values are binding whether they are recognized or not. Holds that governments are obligated to follow and promote these moral values. Sees these values as being clarified in the U.S. Declaration of Independence (see Chapter 16). Is committed to teaching universal moral values in schools. (Abstinence-only sex education would be an example.) Believes that many of the structures of the family, such as sexual faithfulness, are universal moral principles that are to be followed, not redefined. Describes human rights as "inalienable," "inherent," and "God-given."

7. Environmental Catastrophism versus Realism

Transformational Education: Overemphasizes environmental concerns and portrays them in a doomsday light. The role of carbon dioxide in global warming is treated as factual and catastrophic. Population growth is projected to exceed the world's food supply (even though the opposite appears to be true) and genetically modified crops are pictured as being extremely dangerous (even though available information suggests the contrary is true). "Playing it safe" is given priority over scientific knowledge. The West is blamed for the world's environmental worries. Believes that solving the world's environmental problems requires radical changes. Environmental concerns are seen as one of the unifying principles that can motivate people and nations to give up national sovereignty and accept world government. "Sustainable development" is promoted (see Chapter 7). Property rights are redefined or de-emphasized. Pantheism/New Age religion is promoted.

Academic Education: Environmental concerns are recognized but are viewed in a scientific manner. Progress on environmental issues, such as the restoration of Lake Erie, is recognized. Genuine environmental concerns which need attention are also recognized. Most environmental concerns are seen as being the responsibility of national governments as opposed to international government. The role between global warming and carbon dioxide is approached scientifically, not emotionally. Property rights are recognized and protected along with obligations for good stewardship of land and other natural resources. Distinctions are drawn between human beings and plants, animals and the rest of nature. The success of free societies in the West in dealing with environmental issues is recognized. Scientific fact is valued over scare-tactics. A balance between protecting the environment versus the need to supply food and other goods to the people of the world is seen as being desirable.

8. Evolution as Fact versus Teaching the Controversy

Transformational Education: Begins the study of world history with "prehistory" including conjecture about "prehumans" such as Australopithecus and Homo Habilis. Treats evolution as fact—with "fact" defined as the consensus of experts in the field. Defines evolution broadly to include the evolution of government, morality, knowledge and the family. (The New Hampshire Supreme Court acknowledged that it was redefining the family "as it evolves" to include gay marriage.) Our Constitution is viewed as an evolving document. Human rights are pictured as evolving and being, therefore, subject to redefinition. Says that the time has come for the next step of governmental evolution—meaning that the nations of the world must now come together to form a world government.

Academic Education: Believes that history should deal with genuine documents or artifacts, not conjecture or false positions. (Australopithecus, for example, is known to be something other than a missing link between primates and Homo Sapiens.) Proposes that the Darwinism be approached on the basis of actual information, not as consensus. Believes that principles of government, such as inalienable rights, are universal and not subject to evolution. Proposes that the U.S. Constitution be treated on the basis of what it says, not based on rulings of activists courts which place themselves above the Constitution (judicial tyranny). Rejects the notion of "informal" methods of amending the Constitution (by court rulings). Believes that the basic structure of the family is timeless and not subject to evolution. Believes that sovereign nations are essential for protecting individual, inherent rights.

9. Process versus Knowledge

Transformational Education: Emphasizes processes, such as historical thinking, more than historical or geographical knowledge. Knowledge is viewed as being relative to culture, and, for that reason, is seen as being of little importance. Requires students to "analyze," "assess," and "compare" more than asking students to "know" or "understand." This view of education is properly referred to as being process-based, not knowledge-based, and admits that processes are seen as being more important than knowledge.

Academic Education: Emphasizes knowledge and understanding more than processes. Students are seen as needing to analyze and compare, but they are also viewed as being unable to think critically until they have the foundational knowledge upon which to form sound judgments. The goals of teaching traditional subjects such as history and geography are defined primarily in terms of the knowledge students are expected to acquire.

10. Materialism and Pantheism versus Christianity

Transformational Education: Promotes the view that reality consists only of material things (materialism) or promotes pantheism/New Age Religion. Believes that religion evolves. Emphasizes perceived problems for Christianity such as the Crusades, the Inquisition, the Salem witch trials, Darwinism and any hypocrisy of Christian leaders. Christians are typically referred to as "fundamentalists," and are lumped into the same category as cults and Islamic fundamentalists. Christians in politics are pictured as "religious right," "fundamentalists" or "absolutists." Cults, such as the Amish, are pictured as being typical Christians. The positive influence of Christians, such as the role Christians played in the abolition of slavery or the enormous positive influence of Christianity on Western culture is minimized or ignored. An extreme view of the separation of church and state is presented. Christianity is pictured as being hostile to the environment while Eastern religions and pantheism/New

Age theology is pictured as being environmentally friendly. Christianity is pictured as a reason why women are oppressed and as wanting to force its morality on others.

Academic Education: Presents a balanced view of Christianity, being willing to include both its perceived strengths and weaknesses. Rejects the evolution of religion thesis. Acknowledges that the Christian world-view has had a profound influence on Western civilization in general and on the foundational principles of the United States in particular. Generally recognizes the separation of church and state but argues that the First Amendment to the U.S. Constitution limits the federal government, not churches and state governments. Recognizes that the acknowledgment of God is included in the United States system of government and should be distinguished from the "establishment of religion" (creating a state church). Says that home schools and parochial schools should be free from government interference except for safety requirements and for meeting minimum academic expectations.

CHAPTER TWENTY

Criteria for
Civics and Government

Curriculum Guidelines for Civics and Government
Transformational Education versus Academic Education

1. Purpose of Education

Transformational Education: Believes that the purpose of education is to make radical changes in the nature of our people, our government, our basic institutions, our entire society and our world. The Federal Curriculum in civics and government describes schools as training grounds for political activism where the worldview of the new civics is promoted.

Academic Education: Believes that the purpose of education is the transmission of academic knowledge and skills to the next generation. The traditional view has confidence in our basic American institutions and believes that even though these institutions may be modified, they should also be preserved.

2. Teaching Transnational Government versus American Government

Transformational Education: Makes a shift away from the study of the United States to the study of transnational government. (See Appendix H.) So-called "common elements of democracy" are promoted instead of the foundational principles of the United States. The UN's Universal Declaration of Human Rights is described as being superior to the U.S. Bill of Rights and as worthy of any just society. The foundational principles of the United States are pictured as being narrow and dated, while transnational documents, transnational governments and transnational treaties are described as being universal and contemporary, and are said, therefore, to be preferred.

Academic Education: Emphasizes the foundational principles of the United States Government as stated in the Declaration of Independence and the Constitution, especially the Bill of Rights. (See Chapter 16.) These foundational principles of the United States are described as being universal truths, not merely ideas or philosophical goals which are relative to culture. These principles are often referred to as "the American creed." The success of the United States is seen as being largely the result of following these universal principles.

3. The Purpose of Government—Promoting the Common Good versus Protecting the Inalienable Rights

Transformational Education: Describes the purpose of government as twofold—protecting the basic human rights of its people and contributing to the common good. The Preamble of the U.S. Constitution, which mentions both goals, is emphasized instead of the Declaration of Independence. The term "republican" is redefined to mean that promoting the common good is the primary purpose of government. Civic Virtue is emphasized and is defined as sacrificing one's individual rights for the sake of the common good.

Academic Education: Says that the primary purpose of government is protecting the inalienable rights of its people, as stated in the Declaration of Independence and as assumed in the Bill of Rights which is part of the U.S. Constitution. (See Appendix F.) Recognizes that the Preamble to the Constitution is only speaking of the purpose of the Constitution and is not describing the purpose of government. Makes a distinction between totalitarian governments—which make promotion of the common good the primary purpose of government, and the U.S. government—which insists that protecting the inalienable rights is the primary purpose of government. Points out those rights can only be inalienable if protecting them is the primary purpose of government. Civic virtue is defined in terms of the classic virtues such as charity, honesty, industry and temperance.

4. Evolution of Government versus Universal Principles

Transformational Education: Sees government as continually evolving into more advanced forms. Views the Declaration of Independence, therefore, as having been good for Americans 200 years ago but as being obsolete for people today. The Constitution is seen as needing to evolve by means of the decisions of activist courts. The family is also regarded as an evolving institution especially as applied to gay marriage but also as applied to modesty and sexual morality. The UN Declaration of Human Rights is promoted as being more advanced than the U.S. Bill of Rights. Often makes statements like, "The only constant in government is change." Believes that world government is the next logical step in the evolution of government.

Academic Education: Recognizes that government changes, but also recognizes that the inalienable rights and self-evident truths stated in the Declaration of Independence are changeless and not subject to evolution. Includes the recognition of natural law—the universal, changeless principles of morality which govern all human beings and all human institutions. Argues that the reason for the success of the United States is largely the result of its adherence to timeless principles. Believes that freedom and other human rights can only be protected by national governments. Rejects the view that sovereign nations are obsolete and that world government would be superior to sovereign nations.

5. Postmodernism versus Knowledge

Transformational Education: Views academic disciplines as consisting of constructs, not knowledge. Civics and government become the study of different forms of government which are appropriate for different cultures. Students are expected to construct knowledge based on group projects. Constructs are seen as being the interpretations of various cultures; they are not the same as truth or reality. Constructs are pictured as being formed by powerful cultures, or powerful people in those cultures, to keep the vulnerable under control. Mathematics and all other disciples are viewed as being constructs and as requiring deconstruction and reconstruction. Real history is viewed as nonexistent; history is merely the interpretation of the powerful and is used to keep them in power. Knowledge is seen as a consensus of experts. (Radical constructivism, postmodernism and social Marxism of Antonio Gramsci are all accepted terms for this viewpoint.)

Academic Education: Believes that all academic disciplines, including civics and government, contain real knowledge and real truth even though no author is totally objective. Believes that principles of government are knowable, teachable and testable. Also acknowledges the existence of universal principles regarding science, mathematics, psychology, and economics. States that these universal principles are in operation whether they are recognized or not. Emphasizes the transmission of knowledge as being the primary function of education. Recognizes that much of education involves constructs but argues that education also teaches genuine information.

6. Internationalism versus Nationalism

Transformational Education: Emphasizes world citizenship as opposed to national citizenship. Global organizations and treaties are promoted. "Democracy" is redefined to mean power sharing among groups and appointing the top government officials, instead of rule by the people. Supports the continual expansion of the United Nations and its agencies to include, as examples, the International Criminal Court, an international system of education, the new UN standing police force, the UN power to tax and agreements which bring about international control of the environment such as the Kyoto Treaty and the Treaty on Biodiversity. Argues that world government is necessary to solve the various crises in the world today.

Academic Education: Emphasizes the role of nations in the world stage. Protecting inherent rights, controlling pollution, controlling crime and conducting education programs are pictured as being primarily the responsibilities of national governments, not international organizations. The Universal Declaration of Human Rights is viewed as being inferior to the U.S. Bill of Rights because the Bill of Rights acknowledges that basic human rights are inherent and are to be protected by government, while the Universal Declaration of Human Rights sees human rights as being subordinate to the policies of the United Nations. Holds that government has one primary purpose—protecting our unalienable rights. Recognizes that the formation of a world government will lead to the elimination of our national sovereignty and our personal freedom.

7. Relative Morality versus Universal Moral Principles

Transformational Education: Believes that morality is relative to the culture. Marriage, for example, is viewed as a construct of the culture that can be redefined to include gay marriage. Modesty is viewed as cultural construct that can be redefined or eliminated. Human rights like life, liberty and property are viewed as constructs that can be redefined or eliminated. All institutions are viewed as requiring deconstructing and reconstruction. Morality, just like knowledge, is defined as being a consensus of the culture. This consensus is viewed as needing to be changed. The new Masters are seen as being the change-agents for the new world order. Human rights are described as basic, but not as unalienable or God-given.

Academic Education: Sees moral values as universal and as needing to be recognized and followed, not created (Natural Law). Believes that these moral values, such as the right to life, are binding whether they are recognized or not. Holds that governments are obligated to follow these moral values, as clarified in the U.S. Declaration of Independence. Is committed to teaching these moral values in schools. (Abstinence-only sex education—the only type of sex education that works—is an example.) Believes that many of the structures of the family, such as sexual faithfulness, are universal moral principles that are to be followed, not recreated. Defines universal morality to include justice, the golden rule, the rights to life, liberty and property, the right to self-defense, freedom of religion, speech, assembly and conscience. Describes human rights and the moral law as being essentially the same.

8. Environmental Catastrophism versus Progress.

Transformational Education: Overemphasizes environmental concerns and portrays them in a doomsday light. The role of carbon dioxide in global warming is treated as factual and catastrophic. Population growth is projected to exceed the world's food supply (even though the opposite is now known to be true). Genetically modified crops are pictured as being extremely dangerous (even though available information suggests the contrary is true). "Playing it safe" is given priority over scientific knowledge. The Western world is blamed for the world's environmental worries. Agrees that its environmental positions are radical but argues they are necessary. Environmental concerns are seen as one of the unifying principles that can motivate people and nations to give up national sovereignty and accept world government. "Sustainable development" is promoted. (See Chapter 7.) Private property rights are redefined, de-emphasized or opposed. Earth is often viewed in pantheistic/New Age religion concepts.)

Academic Education: Environmental concerns are recognized as being important but are also seen as being manageable. Progress on environmental issues, such as the restoration of Lake Erie, is recognized, along with the need for environmental protection. Most environmental concerns are seen as being the responsibility of national governments as opposed to international government. The role between global warming and carbon dioxide is approached scientifically, not emotionally. Property rights are recognized and protected along with promotion of good stewardship of land and other natural resources. Distinctions are drawn between human beings and plants, animals and the rest of nature. The successes of free societies in the West in dealing with environmental issues are recognized. Scientific fact is valued over scare tactics. A balance is sought between protecting the environment versus economic growth and meeting human needs.

9. Process versus Knowledge

Transformational Education: Emphasizes historical thinking (process) more than historical knowledge (content). Knowledge is viewed as being relative to culture. Requires students to "analyze," "assess," and "compare" more than requiring students to "know" or "understand." This view of education is "process-based."

Academic Education: Emphasizes the acquiring of knowledge and understanding more than processes like historical thinking. Students are seen as needing to analyze and compare, but they are also seen as being unable to analyze and compare, or think critically, until they have the foundational knowledge upon which to form sound judgments. Civics and government are viewed as including information and principles that are knowable, teachable and testable. The study of civics and government is "knowledge-based."

10. Civil Society versus Elected Officials.

Transformational Education: Emphasizes civil society and puts these organizations on a par with elected officials and even with nations. "Civil society" is defined as non-governmental organizations (NGOs). Examples include Planned Parenthood International, Green Cross International, People for the Ethical Treatment of Animals, and the Center for Civic Education (CCE). (Liberal NGOs are commonly funded by large foundations such as the Ford Foundation and the Rockefeller Foundation as well as by government grants.) NGOs are given substantial authority; they play influential roles in writing international treaties including the Treaty on Biodiversity, in writing international statements of policy, such as the Earth Charter, and in writing the *National Standards For Civics and Government.* Recommendations for UN "reform" call for even greater influence for NGOs.

Academic Education: Believes that elected officials and elected governments should have far greater authority and influence than NGOs. Observes that members of NGOs never face public elections and, therefore, are not accountable to the public. Also observes that NGOs are special interest groups which are not obligated to present the views of the majority of voters and do not normally provide research or recommend polices that are objective or balanced. Opposes giving NGOs, such as the Center for Civic Education, the authority to write the Federal Curriculum (*National Standards for Civics and Government*). Believes that curriculum decisions should be made by elected officials at the state and local levels and by local schools. Recognizes the undue influence of large foundations with left-leaning agendas.

CHAPTER TWENTY-ONE

Criteria for Language Arts

D avid Horowitz and others have said that language arts is now the preferred subject area used by the left for teaching its political and ideological agenda. For that reason all of the criteria described above also apply to language arts. Language arts may be the most difficult area to evaluate because the teaching of ideology in literature is done indirectly. Indirect indoctrination, however, is just as effective as direct indoctrination.

Curriculum Guidelines for Language Arts
Transformational Education versus Academic Education

1. Subject matter

Transformational Education: Assumes that the Federal Curriculum (the themes of all the national standards) will be taught in the language arts classes. The civics and government curriculum forms the core-curriculum for language arts as it also does for the national standards. Literature selections are made primarily because they teach the themes of the Federal Curriculum, not because they are good literature and not because they are useful pedagogically. See for example, the literature recommended by the National Council for the Social Studies (NCSS) in its *Children's Literature in Social Studies: Teaching to the Standards* (Washington D.C.: NCSS) 1998. (No selections are included in the NCSS recommendations with copyrights older than 1990; the classics have been eliminated. Tables at the end of the NCSS recommendations identify which of the Federal Curriculum themes are taught by each of the recommended selections.) Includes the reading of technical materials which is part of the School-to-Work system.

Academic Education: Believes that the primary purpose of language arts is the teaching of language arts skills. Literature selections are made primarily because of the quality of the literature and its pedagogical usefulness. Recognizes that the reading of good literature is essential so that students learn to enjoy reading. Rejects the position that literature should be chosen because of its promotion of a particular worldview. The literature selections, as a whole, are viewed as being consistent with the prevailing views of Western civilization.

2. Phonics versus Whole Language

Transformational Education: Promotes the whole language approach to the teaching of reading or, more commonly, claims to present a combination of phonics and whole language.

Academic Education: Recognizes that phonics has proven to be the superior methodology for teaching reading, and, for that reason, uses a phonics-based approach.

3. Teaching the Mechanics of Language

Transformational Education: Downplays the teaching of spelling, punctuation, grammar, and paragraph structure. Promotes "creative spelling" and "creative grammar" instead. Focuses on the supposed creativity of the child instead of teaching correct mechanics. Norms of mechanics are viewed as cultural constructs and are seen as being of little importance and even as an impediment to creativity. Because of the time dedicated to teaching the themes of the Federal Curriculum, relatively little time is available for teaching the mechanics of language.

Academic Education: Believes in teaching correct spelling, punctuation, and sentence structure. Also teaches the principles of sentence and paragraph composition and composition generally. Recognizes that while many of the structures of language are constructs, there are also universal principles of language and communications that need to be taught and applied to writing and speaking. Sets high standards for accuracy on performance of mechanical skills.

4. Multiculturalism

Transformational Education: Includes large numbers of literature selections which teach the principles of radical multiculturalism (see

Chapter 5). Literary selections involve members of minority communities by a ratio of at least double their frequency in the population. No selections are included that describe minority communities in a negative light. Few classics are included in the literature selections.

Academic Education: Literature selections are made primarily on the basis of literary merit and pedagogical usefulness. Literature selections will include authors and characters from minority communities, but the choice of such literature is made on the basis of merit. Literary selections include numerous classics.

5. Postmodernism and New Marxism

Transformational Education: Emphasizes literature which provides "multiple perspectives" on a given topic. Suggests that "knowledge" is merely a matter of a culture's point of view, not a matter of reality or truth. Divides all cultures and other groups into two categories—the oppressor group and the oppressed group. Homosexuality is promoted. Morality and modesty are reduced to being cultural constructs. Traditional American heroes are commonly portrayed in a negative light. Heroes from other countries are consistently portrayed in a positive light. Group projects are emphasized to promote group consciousness and group identity as opposed to individual consciousness and identity.

Academic Education: Includes literary selections that teach American history, that are patriotic and that highlight national heroes. History is viewed as being knowable, teachable and testable. Morality is pictured as being genuine and universal. Grammar and punctuation are viewed as being correct for the nation or group of nations. Individualism is portrayed in a positive light. Individual work is highlighted, and students are graded on individual performance.

6. New Age/Pantheism

Transformational Education: Includes a significant number of selections describing the mythology of pagan religions (see Chapter 8). Much of the mythology is included in pre-school and elementary school literature. Religions and religious practices of other cultures are highlighted and pictured in a positive light. Eastern religions and Islam are included. Nature is pictured as "Mother Nature" and as "Mother Earth." Trees and animals are viewed as being brothers and sisters with human beings. Christianity is described in negative terms including one-sided depictions of the Crusades, Inquisition and Salem Witch Trials. Groups such as the Amish are described as being representative of Christianity. Conservative Christians are put in the same category with Islamic extremists and are pictured as being equally dangerous.

Academic Education: Chooses literature based on its merits and pedagogical usefulness, not because it promotes a particular religion or worldview.

7. Feminism versus Traditional Families

Transformational Education: Girls and women are primarily portrayed in non-traditional roles. Two-parent families are rarely included. Literature describing traditional marriage is seldom included. If marriage is included, it is usually pictured as being oppressive to women. Females are generally pictured in a positive light, while white males are pictured in a mostly negative light. Males are viewed as exploiting women. Differences between males and females are viewed as being the result of conditioning only. Morality and modesty are pictured as cultural constructs which have a negative, constraining influence on women.

Academic Education: Literature is chosen for its quality, not for its advocacy of a particular worldview. As a consequence girls and women are pictured in a variety of roles. Because the world is pictured realistically, men and women are viewed as having both positive and negative characteristics. The complementary nature of gender roles is recognized. Marriage is pictured in a mostly positive light. Marriage is viewed as being the oneness of a man and a women and is viewed as forming the ideal basis for the family. Most families are portrayed as having two parents. Morality is pictured as having universal characteristics. Modesty is seen as being real and more than mere cultural preference. Realistic romance is included.

8. Sustainable Development

Transformational Education: Environmental concerns are highlighted and are pictured as being catastrophic. Subject matter which encourages emotional involvement in environmental issues is featured. Pantheism is promoted (see Chapters 6, 7 & 8). Social and political activism are encouraged. Oneness with nature, oneness of all existence and being brothers and sisters with plants and animals are featured.

Loggers are pictured as villains. Hunting is pictured as being morally wrong. The agricultural use of commercial fertilizers, genetically modified crops and the use of chemicals are pictured as harmful. Private ownership of property is viewed negatively. Unity with nature as opposed to wise management of nature is promoted. Nature is pictured as being the steward of human beings, not the other way around.

Academic Education: Literature is selected on the basis of its merit, not because it promotes an agenda. Environmental concerns are portrayed realistically; they will not be exaggerated, nor will they consist of emotional manipulation. People are viewed as having critical differences as compared to nonhumans. Good management of nature by people is included. Honest vocations including logging and agriculture are pictured in a positive light. The Judeo-Christian view of nature is more likely to be included than the pagan, pantheistic or Eastern religion views.

9. Globalism versus Nationalism

Transformational Education: People are described as being naturally cooperative and peace loving. The United States is pictured as an imperialistic power which exploits other countries for its own advantage. Nationalism is described in terms of the exaggerated nationalism of Nazi Germany. War is viewed as the result of nationalism and imperialism of strong countries including the United States. All cultures are viewed as being equal except that the United States is seen as being inferior. All religions are pictured as being equal except for Christianity which is defined in negative terms. The United States is described as being responsible for the terrorist attacks used against it as well as being responsible for terrorism in general. International activities and organizations are included and viewed in a positive light.

Academic Education: Literature is chosen for its merit, not because it promotes a particular political, religious or ideological point of view. The exceptionalism of the West generally and of the United States in particular is recognized. Selections which include recognition of original sin are included. Nationalism and patriotism are pictured in a normal, positive way. The national identity and unique culture of the United States are recognized. Selections describing American heroes are included. Themes which are part of the Twelve Pillars of Freedom are presented in the literature.

CHAPTER TWENTY-TWO

Criteria for Math and Science

Curriculum Guidelines for Mathematics and Science
Transformational Education versus Academic Education

1. Definition of Science

Transformational Education: Defines "science" as being more of a learning process than a body of knowledge. The goal of science education becomes "scientific inquiry" or "scientific literacy" as opposed to the mastery of scientific knowledge and skills. The term "scientific law" is de-emphasized; terms like "models" and "concepts" of science are preferred. Particular emphasis is placed on scientific concepts that are immediately relevant to the student's everyday life. Such science is called "authentic." Science is defined in naturalistic terms so that the supernatural is ruled out by definition.

Academic Education: Sees that science is a body of knowledge as well as a system of methodologies. Is more likely to emphasize the scientific method as opposed to the broader and more loosely defined term "scientific inquiry." Emphasizes scientific laws as opposed to mere models and concepts. Views math and science education as the transmission of an objective body of knowledge and skills which may or may not seem relevant to the immediate life of the student. Defines science in naturalistic terms, but does not rule out the supernatural by definition. Is open to scientific debate on a wide variety of subjects including evolution.

2. Political Activism

Transformational Education: Defines science education to include political activism. Organizes science education around a three-fold sequence described by (a) knowledge-related verbs such as "understand," then proceeds (b) to process-type verbs, such as "evaluate," and ends with (c) action-oriented verbs, such as "plan" or "develop." Some of the action-oriented verbs involve political and social activism. Political actions dealing with environmental issues are favorite topics. Treats morality as being universal and absolute when dealing with environmental issues but not when dealing with other issues. May allege that Christianity is partially responsible for a supposed environmental crisis. Advocates the broad ideological and political agenda of sustainable development as defined by the Earth Charter (see Chapter 7).

Academic Education: Rejects the view that political activism should be part of science education. Takes a liberal arts approach to education which recognizes that information may suggest actions, but such actions are seen as being the free choice of students. States that science education should be knowledge-based and academic, not activism-oriented. Believes that any activism should be based on objective scientific research and knowledge. Avoids using scare tactics on any issue.

3. Definition of Knowledge

Transformational Education: Assumes a postmodernist view of knowledge; "knowledge" is defined as the consensus of experts in the field at a given point in time. "Knowledge" is not seen as being true. The terms "knowledge" and "scientific law" are used, but they are redefined to mean constructs (the way a particular culture looks at things at a particular time), not as being reality. So-called Western constructs are often viewed as being racist and sexist. Little emphasis is placed on learning factual information, such as laws, theorems, and formulas, because facts are viewed as being useful concepts but not as being reality. Emphasizes the evolution of knowledge. Emphasizes the view of multiple intelligences.

Academic Education: Rejects postmodernism and regards the transmission of academic knowledge and skills as being the primary goal of education. Recognizes that scientific theories are continually being improved, but avoids separating science and mathematics from truth and reality. Believes that truth exists objectively. Sees science as being nonpolitical, nonideological and nonreligious. Believes that truth can be discovered, quantified, communicated to others and tested. Defines student achievement in science and mathematics as the acquisition of knowledge and skills. Recognizes the importance of memorizing certain basic facts including computation skills.

4. Integrated Math

Transformational Education: Supports the National Council of Teachers of Mathematics (NCTM) math which is essentially the same as integrated math. Emphasizes the significance of the national standards of mathematics and the need to standardize math education nationwide. Opposes traditional math such as Saxon math. Follows the constructivist philosophy that knowledge is formulated by the student, not taught to the student. Also follows the postmodernist and new Marxist views which see math as a mere construct which has no necessary relationship with the real world. Math is "integrated" into the world of the student as opposed to being studied by itself. De-emphasizes rote memorization, including the learning of basic arithmetic, in favor of using calculators and "discovery learning" where students figure out formulas and methodologies for themselves. Minimizes the use of word problems having predetermined outcomes. Emphasizes group projects and group grading. Supports teaching of civics and government, as defined by the national standards, in both math and science classes.

Academic Education: Uses the traditional math philosophy in determining content, teaching sequences and methodology. Emphasizes arithmetic including memorizing basic computation tables. Includes extensive practice and repetitions of basic concepts. Sees math as corresponding to the real world. Recognizes the value of lectures and factual material along with the active engagement of students. Believes that many math and science principles can effectively be taught by themselves. Sees the value of discovery learning but also recognizes that it is relatively inefficient in teaching math and science content. Emphasizes individual work and individual grading over group activities. Rejects the view that political themes should be taught in math and science. Follows a liberal arts approach to knowledge by allowing scientific information to speak for itself regardless of its application to political policies. Recognizes that NCTM math fails to give students adequate preparation for college-level mathematics.

5. Evolution

Transformational Education: Believes that evolution is a matter of scientific fact and knowledge, not a working hypothesis. Defines evolution broadly to include the evolution of life, morality, the universe, knowledge, the family, all social institutions and government. Includes as "proofs" of evolution various examples that have been discredited. Examples used to "prove" evolution include peppered moths, Haeckel's embryos, Australopithecus as a supposed ancestor of Homo Sapiens, and several alleged missing links between dinosaurs and birds. Makes evolution the central explanatory paradigm of all science including social science.

Academic Education: Views evolution as a working hypothesis, not as a matter of fact or knowledge. Admits to major gaps in evolutionary theory, such as the gaps between life and non-life, between primates and man, and between dinosaurs and birds. Recognizes the circularity of argument in many of the explanations offered by evolution. Admits to the disagreements among evolutionists regarding various aspects of the theory. Rejects the view that the intelligent design theory is outside the definition of science and is unscientific by definition. Realizes the difficulties involved in reconciling naturalistic evolution with human experiences such as the existence of morality.

6. Sustainable Development

Transformational Education: Promotes the ideological worldview and political agenda of sustainable development as defined by the Earth Charter (see Chapter 7). Overemphasizes environmental issues. Views global warming as scientific, man-made, undesirable and catastrophic. Emphasizes potential dangers of genetically modified (GMO) crops. Continues to advocate the Malthusian view that the world's population will increase faster than the world's food supply. Overemphasizes ecosystems. Supports man's living in harmony with nature as opposed to being managers of nature. Prefers scare tactics and takes a doomsday approach to environmental issues instead of obtaining adequate scientific data before making judgments. Tends to oppose private property rights.

Academic Education: Emphasizes obtaining sufficient scientific information prior to proposing changes in environmental policy. Strikes a balance between environmental concerns and human needs. Recognizes progress made on environmental issues as well as the reality of environmental problems. Understands that the world's food supply continues to grow faster than the population. Sees that the low birth-rate is now a substantial problem in many areas of the world. Appreciates the green revolution, the development and use of GMO crops, and the value of the wise use of commercial fertilizer and agricultural chemicals. Is cautious about making sweeping judgments about any role of carbon dioxide emissions on the world's climate. Promotes the wise management of nature as opposed to living in harmony with nature. Supports private property rights and free enterprise.

7. Multiculturalism

Transformational Education: Makes political multiculturalism (also called "diversity") a part of math and science education. Promotes what it calls "multicultural mathematics." Minimizes the role the West has played over the past 500 years in giving rise to the scientific revolution. Includes contributions to science by members of minority communities because of their minority community membership, not because of the value of the scientific contribution. Promotes looking at math and science from "multiple perspectives." Uses the formula which requires that any narratives or images of people involved in scientific endeavors must include minority members in a frequency that is double their occurrence in the population.

Academic Education: Opposes including radical multiculturalism in science education. Is not embarrassed or apologetic about the dominant role played by Western civilization in the rise of science over the past 500 years. Views such issues as being matters of science, not politics. Recognizes the positive contribution that Western culture generally, including religions such as Christianity, has played in the rise of science. Recognizes the contributions various individuals have made to science on the basis of the value of the contributions, not on the basis of political or ideological quotas or objectives.

8. Birth Control, Bio-Ethics and Sex Education

Transformational Education: Eager to experiment with human cloning, gene splicing involving human cells, stem-cell research and human genetics generally. Recognizes no moral restraints on such experimentation. Sees no essential differences between human life and other forms of life. Supports artificial insemination and abortion as a means of supposedly improving the human race. Hopes to help evolution along by creating a new, more advanced form of human beings. Promotes "value-free" sex education.

Academic Education: Recognizes moral restraints involved in sexual activity and in experimentation with human embryos and human genes. Believes there are essential differences between animal sexuality and human sexuality. Opposes eugenics (the attempt to create a master race). Has a high view of human life and recognizes the right to life as being a universal, inherent right of all people. Sees the relationship between Western culture and the protection of individual human life. Believes that human life has higher value than non-human life. Evaluates sex education on the basis of what works to reduce illicit sexual activity, unwanted pregnancy and sexually transmitted diseases, and for that reason recognizes that abstinence-only sex education is the only method that produces positive outcomes.

Appendices

Liberal Democracy vs. Transnational Progressivism:

THE FUTURE OF THE IDEOLOGICAL CIVIL WAR WITHIN THE WEST

By John Fonte

Nearly a year before the September 11 attacks on the World Trade Center and the Pentagon, wire service stories gave us a preview of the transnational politics of the future. It was reported on October 24, 2000, that in preparation for the UN Conference Against Racism, about fifty American nongovernmental organizations (NGOs) sent a formal letter to UN Human Rights Commissioner Mary Robinson calling on the UN "to hold the United States accountable for the intractable and persistent problem of discrimination" that "men and women of color face at the hands of the U.S. criminal justice system."[1]

The NGOs included the Leadership Conference on Civil Rights, Amnesty International-U. S.A. (AI-U.S.A.), Human Rights Watch (HRW), the Arab-American Institute, National Council of Churches, American Friends Service Committee, the National Association for the Advancement of Colored People, the American Civil Liberties Union, the Mexican-American Legal Defense and Educational Fund, the International Human Rights Law Group, the Lawyers Committee for Civil Rights under Law, and others. Their spokesman, Wade Henderson, of the Leadership Conference on Civil Rights, stated that the NGOs' demands "had been repeatedly raised with federal and state officials [in the United States] but to little effect. . . . In frustration we now turn to the United Nations."[2] In other words, the NGOs, unable to enact the policies they favored through the normal processes of American constitutional democracy-the Congress, state governments, state courts, the federal executive branch, or even the federal courts-felt it necessary to appeal to authority outside of American democracy and beyond its Constitution.

In the two weeks before September 11, from August 31 to September 7, 2001, the UN World Conference against Racism, Racial Discrimination, Xenophobia, and Related Intolerance was held in Durban, South Africa. The American NGOs listed above attended the conference with financial support from the Ford, Rockefeller, MacArthur, and Charles Stewart Mott Foundations. At the conference the NGOs worked with delegates from African states that supported "reparations" from Western nations as compensation for the transatlantic slave trade of the seventeenth to nineteenth centuries. American NGOs provided research assistance and helped develop reparations resolutions that condemned only the West, without mentioning the larger traffic in African slaves that were sent to the Islamic lands of the Middle East. In addition, the NGOs endorsed a series of demands, including:

- U.S. acknowledgment of "the breadth and pervasiveness of institutional racism" that "permeates every institution at every level."
- A declaration that "racial bias corrupts every stage of the [U.S.] criminal justice process, from suspicion to investigation, arrest, prosecution, trial, and sentencing."
- Support and expansion of federal and state hate crimes legislation.
- Condemnation of opposition to affirmative action measures.
- U.S. recognition of an adequate standard of living as a "right, not privilege."
- A statement deploring "denial of economic rights" in the United States.
- Promotion of multilingualism instead of "discriminatory" English-language acquisition emphasis in U.S. schools.
- Denunciation of free market capitalism as a fundamentally flawed system."[3]

Most importantly, the NGOs insisted that the United States ratify all major UN human rights treaties and drop legal reservations to treaties already ratified. For example, in 1994 the United States ratified the UN Convention on the Elimination of Racial Discrimination (CERD), but attached reservations declaring that it did not accept treaty requirements "incompatible with the Constitution." The official State Department reservations memorandum specifically notes that the CERD's restrictions on free speech and freedom of assembly are incompatible with the First Amendment. Yet leading NGOs including the HRW and AI-U.S.A. demand that the United States drop all reservations and "comply" with the CERD treaty.[4]

On August 6, 2001, Reuters reported that the United States had presented its first explanation of how it was implementing the CERD treaty to a UN committee. An NGO representative from the Center for Constitutional Rights reportedly said that "Almost every member of the UN committee raised the question of why there are vast racial disparities...in every aspect of American life-education, housing, health, welfare, criminal justice." A representative from HRW declared that the United States offered "no remedies" for these disparities, but "simply restated" its position by supporting equality of opportunity and indicating "no willingness to comply" with CERD.[5] (This would presumably mean the enactment of policies resulting in statistical equality of condition for racial and ethnic minorities in education, housing, health, welfare, criminal justice and the like.)

Indeed, to comply with the NGO interpretation of the CERD treaty, the United States would have to turn its political and economic system, together with their underlying principles, upside down-abandoning the free speech guarantees of the Constitution, bypassing federalism, and ignoring the very concept of majority rule-since practically nothing in the NGO agenda is supported by the American electorate.

The NGOs at the Durban conference exemplify a new challenge to liberal democracy and its traditional home, the liberal democratic nation-state. These have always been self-governing representative systems comprised of individual citizens who enjoy freedom and equality under law and together form a people within a democratic nation-state. Thus, liberal democracy means individual rights, democratic representation (with some form of majority rule) and national citizenship. Yet, as the vignettes of the Durban conference (and myriad other conflicts of the past four decades) demonstrate, all of these principles, along with the very idea of the liberal democratic nation-state, are contested today in the West, suggesting that we have not reached the "end of history" in the ideological sense delineated by Francis Fukuyama in his groundbreaking 1989 essay.[6]

POST-SEPTEMBER 11

Three weeks after the September 11 attacks, Fukuyama stated in an article in the *Wall Street Journal* that his "end of history" thesis remained valid twelve years after he first presented it, shortly before the fall of the Berlin Wall. Fukuyama's core argument was that after the defeat of communism and National Socialism, no serious ideological competitor to Western-style liberal democracy was likely to emerge in the future. Thus, in terms of political philosophy, liberal democracy is the end of the evolutionary process. To be sure, there will be wars and terrorism, but no alternative ideology with a universal appeal will seriously challenge the ideas and values of Western liberal democracy as the "dominant organizing principles" around the world.

Fukuyama correctly points out that non-democratic rival ideologies such as radical Islam and "Asian values" have little appeal outside their own cultural areas, but these areas are themselves vulnerable to penetration by Western democratic ideas. The September 11 attacks notwithstanding, "we remain at the end of history," Fukuyama insists, "because there is only one system that will continue to dominate world politics, that of the liberal-democratic West." There is nothing beyond liberal democracy "towards which we could expect to evolve." Fukuyama concludes by stating that there will be challenges from those who resist progress, "but time and resources are on the side of modernity."[7]

Indeed, but is "modernity" on the side of liberal democracy? Fukuyama is probably right that the current crisis with the forces of radical Islam will be overcome, and that, at the end of the day, there will be no serious ideological challenge originating outside of Western civilization. However, the activities of the NGOs suggest that there already is an alternative ideology to liberal democracy within the West that for decades has been steadily, and almost imperceptibly, evolving.

Thus, it is entirely possible that modernity thirty or forty years hence will witness not the final triumph of liberal democracy, but a new challenge to it in the form of a new transnational hybrid regime that is post-liberal democratic, and in the context of the American republic, post-Constitutional and post-American. I will call this alternative ideology "transnational progressivism." This ideology constitutes a universal and modern worldview that challenges in theory and practice both the liberal democratic nation-state in general and the American regime in particular. The aftermath of September 11 provides the possibility of a resurgence by the forces of traditional nation-centered liberal democracy. But before addressing this possibility, it is necessary to examine in detail the theory and practice of "transnational progressivism."

TRANSNATIONAL PROGRESSIVISM

The key concepts of transnational progressivism could be described as follows:

(1) *The ascribed group over the individual citizen.* The key political unit is not the individual citizen, who forms voluntary associations

and works with fellow citizens regardless of race, sex, or national origin, but the ascriptive group (racial, ethnic, or gender) into which one is born. This emphasis on race, ethnicity, and gender leads to group consciousness and a deemphasis of the individual's capacity for choice and for transcendence of ascriptive categories, joining with others beyond the confines of social class, tribe, and gender to create a cohesive nation.

(2) *A dichotomy of groups: Oppressor vs. victim groups, with immigrant groups designated as victims.* Influenced (however indirectly) by the Hegelian Marxist thinking associated with the Italian writer Antonio Gramsci (1891-1937) and the Central European theorists known as the Frankfurt School, global progressives posit that throughout human history there are essentially two types of groups: the oppressor and the oppressed, the privileged and the marginalized. In the United States, oppressor groups would variously include white males, heterosexuals, and Anglos, whereas victim groups would include blacks, gays, Latinos including obviously many immigrants), and women.

Multicultural ideologists have incorporated this essentially Hegelian Marxist "privileged vs. marginalized" dichotomy into their theoretical framework. As political philosopher James Ceaser puts it, multiculturalism is not "multi" or concerned with many groups, but "binary," concerned with two groups, the hegemon (bad) and "the Other" (good) or the oppressor and the oppressed. Thus, in global progressive ideology, "equity" and "social justice" mean strengthening the position of the victim groups and weakening the position of oppressors-hence preferences for certain groups are justified. Accordingly, equality under law is replaced by legal preferences for traditionally victimized groups. In 1999, the U.S. Equal Employment Opportunity Commission extended antidiscrimination protection under Title VII of the 1964 Civil Rights Act to illegal immigrants.

(3) *Group proportionalism as the goal of "fairness."* Transnational progressivism assumes that "victim" groups should be represented in all professions roughly proportionate to their percentage of the population or, at least, of the local work force. Thus, if women make up 52 percent and Latinos make up 10 percent of the population, then 52 percent of all corporate executives, physicians, and insurance salesmen should be women and 10 percent should be Latinos. If not, there is a problem of "underrepresentation" or imbalance that must be rectified by government and civil society. Thomas Sowell recently wrote-as he has for several decades-that

many Western intellectuals perpetually promote some version of "cosmic justice" or form of equality of result.[8] The "group proportionalism" paradigm is pervasive in Western society: even the U.S. Park Service is concerned because 85 percent of all visitors to the nation's parks are white, although whites make up only 74 percent of the population. Therefore, the Park Service announced in 1998 that it was working on this "problem."[9]

(4) *The values of all dominant institutions to be changed to reflect the perspectives of the victim groups.* Transnational progressives in the United States (and elsewhere) insist that it is not enough to have proportional representation of minorities (including immigrants, legal and illegal) at all levels in major institutions of society (corporations, places of worship, universities, armed forces) if these institutions continue to reflect a "white Anglo male culture and world view." Ethnic and linguistic minorities have different ways of viewing the world, they say, and these minorities' values and cultures must be respected and represented within these institutions. At a 1998 U.S. Department of Education conference promoting bilingual education, SUNY professor Joel Spring declared, "We must use multiculturalism and multilingualism to change the dominant culture of the United States." He noted, for example, that unlike Anglo culture, Latino culture is "warm" and would not promote harsh disciplinary measures in the schools.[10]

(5) *The Demographic Imperative.* The demographic imperative tells us that major demographic changes are occurring in the United States as millions of new immigrants from non-Western cultures and their children enter American life in record numbers. At the same time, the global interdependence of the world's peoples and the transnational connections among them will increase. All of these changes render the traditional paradigm of American nationhood obsolete. That traditional paradigm based on individual rights, majority rule, national sovereignty, citizenship, and the assimilation of immigrants into an existing American civic culture is too narrow and must be changed into a system that promotes "diversity," defined, in the end, as group proportionalism.

(6) *The redefinition of democracy and "democratic ideals."* Since Fukayama's treatise, transnational progressives have been altering the definition of "democracy," from that of a system of majority rule among equal citizens to one of power sharing among ethnic groups composed of both citizens and non-citizens. For example,

Mexican foreign minister Jorge Castañeda wrote in the Atlantic Monthly in July 1995 that it is "undemocratic" for California to exclude noncitizens, specifically illegal aliens, from voting. Former Immigration and Naturalization Service (INS) general counsel Alexander Aleinikoff, declaring that "[we] live in a post-assimilationist age," asserted that majority preferences simply "reflect the norms and cultures of dominant groups" (as opposed to the norms and cultures of "feminists and people of color").[11] James Banks, one of American education's leading textbook writers, noted in 1994 that "to create an authentic democratic Unum with moral authority and perceived legitimacy the pluribus (diverse peoples) must negotiate and share power."[12] In effect, Banks said, existing American liberal democracy is not quite authentic; real democracy is yet to be created. It will come when the different "peoples" or groups that live within America "share power" as groups.

(7) *Deconstruction of national narratives and national symbols.*
Transnational progressives have focused on traditional narratives and national symbols of Western democratic nation-states, questioning union and nationhood itself. In October 2000, the British government-sponsored Commission on the Future of Multi-Ethnic Britain issued a report that denounced the concept of "Britishness" as having "systemic . . . racist connotations." The Commission, chaired by Labour life peer Lord Parekh, declared that instead of defining itself as a nation, the UK should be considered a "community of communities." One member of the Commission explained that the members found the concepts of "Britain" and "nation" troubling. The purpose of the Commission's report, according to the chairman Professor Parekh, was to "shape and restructure the consciousness of our citizens." The report declared that Britain should be formally "recognized as a multi-cultural society" whose history needed to be "revised, rethought, or jettisoned."[13]

In the United States in the mid-1990s, the proposed "National History Standards," reflecting the marked influence of multiculturalism among historians in the nation's universities, recommended altering the traditional narrative of the United States. Instead of emphasizing the story of European settlers, American civilization would be redefined as a "convergence" of three civilizations-Amerindian, West African, and European-the bases of a hybrid American multiculture. Even though the National History Standards were ultimately rejected, this core multicultural concept that that United States is not primarily the creation of Western civilization, but the result of a "Great Convergence" of "three worlds" has become the dominant paradigm in American public schools.

In Israel, adversary intellectuals have attacked the Zionist narrative. A "post-Zionist" intelligentsia has proposed that Israel consider itself multicultural and deconstruct its identity as a Jewish state. Tom Bethell has pointed out that in the mid-1990s the official appointed to revise Israel's history curriculum used media interviews to compare the Israeli armed forces to the SS and Orthodox Jewish youth to the Hitler Youth. A new code of ethics for the Israel Defense Forces eliminated all references to the "land of Israel," the "Jewish state," and the "Jewish people," and, instead, referred only to "democracy." Even Israeli foreign minister Simon Peres sounded the post-Zionist trumpet in his 1993 book, The New Middle East, where he wrote that "we do not need to reinforce sovereignty, but rather to strengthen the position of humankind." He called for an "ultranational identity," saying that "particularist nationalism is fading and the idea of a 'citizen of the world' is taking hold. . . . Our ultimate goal is the creation of a regional community of nations, with a common market and elected centralized bodies," a type of Middle Eastern EU.[14]

(8) *Promotion of the concept of postnational citizenship.* "Can advocates of postnational citizenship ultimately succeed in decoupling the concept of citizenship from the nation-state in prevailing political thought?" asks Rutgers Law Professor Linda Bosniak.[15] An increasing number of international law professors throughout the West are arguing that citizenship should be denationalized. Invoking concepts such as inclusion, social justice, democratic engagement, and human rights, they argue for transnational citizenship, postnational citizenship, or sometimes global citizenship embedded in international human rights accords and "evolving" forms of transnational arrangements.

These theorists insist that national citizenship should not be "privileged" at the expense of postnational, multiple, and pluralized forms of citizenship identities. For example, the Carnegie Endowment for International Peace, under the leadership of its president, Jessica Tuchman Mathews, has published a series of books in the past few years "challenging traditional understandings of belonging and membership" in nation-states and "rethinking the meaning of citizenship."[16] Although couched in the ostensibly neutral language of social science, these essays from scholars from Germany, Britain, Canada, and France, as well as the United States, argue for new, transnational forms of citizenship as a normative good.

(9) *The idea of transnationalism as a major conceptual tool.* The theory of transnationalism promises to be for the first decade of the twenty-first century what multiculturalism was for the last decade of the twentieth century. In a certain sense, transnationalism is the next stage of multicultural ideology-it is multiculturalism with a global face. Like multiculturalism, transnationalism is a concept that provides elites with both an empirical tool (a plausible analysis of what is) and an ideological framework (a vision of what should be). Transnational advocates argue that globalization requires some form of transnational "global governance" because they believe that the nation-state and the idea of national citizenship are ill suited to deal with the global problems of the future. Academic and public policy conferences today are filled with discussions of "transnational organizations," "transnational actors," "transnational migrants," "transnational jurisprudence," and "transnational citizenship," just as in the 1990s they were replete with references to multiculturalism in education, citizenship, literature, and law.

Many of the same scholars who touted multiculturalism now herald the coming transnational age. Thus, at its August 1999 annual conference, "Transitions in World Societies," the same American Sociological Association (ASA) that promoted multiculturalism from the late 1980s to the mid-1990s featured transnationalism. Indeed, the ASA's then-president, Professor Alejandro Portes of Princeton University, argued that transnationalism is the wave of the future.He insisted that transnationalism, combined with large-scale immigration, would redefine the meaning of American citizenship. University of Chicago anthropologist Arjun Appadurai has suggested that the United States is in transition from being a "land of immigrants" to "one node in a postnational network of diasporas."[17]

It is clear that arguments over globalization will dominate much of early twenty-first century public debate. The promotion of transnationalism as both an empirical and normative concept is an attempt to shape this crucial intellectual struggle over globalization. The adherents of transnationalism create a dichotomy. They imply that one is either in step with globalization, and thus with transnationalism and forward-looking thinking, or one is a backward antiglobalist. Liberal democrats (who are internationalists and support free trade and market economics) must reply that this is a false dichotomy-that the critical argument is not between globalists and antiglobalists, but instead over the form Western global engagement should take in the coming decades: will it be transnationalist or internationalist?

Transnational Progressivism's Social Base: A Post-National Intelligentsia

The social base of transnational progressivism could be labeled a rising postnational intelligentsia, the leaders of which include many international law professors at prestigious Western universities, NGO activists, foundation officers, UN bureaucrats, EU administrators, corporation executives, and practicing politicians throughout the West. The postnational intelligentsia is an eclectic group but it would include an identifiable group of thinkers and actors.

- British "third way" theorist Anthony Giddens, who declared that he is "in favor of pioneering some quasi-utopian transnational forms of democracy" and "is strongly opposed to the idea that social justice is just equality of opportunity."[18] Giddens writes that "the shortcomings of liberal democracy suggest the need to further more radical forms of democratization." Instead of liberal democracy, Giddens, using the language of Juergen Habermas, posits a "dialogic democracy" with an emphasis on "life politics," especially "new social movements, such as those concerned with feminism, ecology, peace, or human rights."[19]
- Italian Marxist theorist Toni Negri (who clearly knows his Gramsci) and Duke University Literature Professor Michael Hardt, the authors of the best-selling book Empire, lauded by the *New York Times* as the "next big idea."
- In *Empire*, Negri (a jailed former associate of the terrorist Italian Red Brigades) and Hardt (his former student) using Marxist concepts such as the "multitudes" i.e., "the masses" vs. the Empire attack the power of global corporations and, without being overly specific, call for a new form of "global" or transnational democracy.
- University of Chicago philosophy professor Martha Nussbaum, who called for reinvigorating the concept of "global citizenship" and denounced patriotism as indistinguishable from jingoism" in a debate several years back that set off a wide-ranging discussion among American academics on the meaning of patriotism, citizenship, and the nation-state.[20]

166

- Strobe Talbot, former undersecretary of state, who wrote when he was an editor of *Time* magazine in the early 1990's that he was optimistic that by the end of the twenty-first century "nationhood as we know it will be obsolete: all states will recognize a single global authority....All countries are basically social arrangements, accommodations to changing circumstances. No matter how permanent and even sacred they may seem at any one time, in fact they are all artificial and temporary." He characterizes the devolution of national sovereignty "upward toward supranational bodies" and "downward toward" autonomous units is a "basically positive phenomenon."[21]

Complementary to this general (and diffuse) sentiment for new transnational forms of governance is the concrete day-to-day practical work of the NGOs that seek to bring the transnational vision to fruition. When social movements such as the ideologies of "transnationalism" and "global governance" are depicted as the result of "social forces" or the "movement of history," a certain impersonal inevitability is implied. However, in the twentieth century the Bolshevik Revolution, the National Socialist Revolution, the New Deal, the Reagan Revolution, the Gaullist national reconstruction in France, and the creation of the EU and its predecessor organizations were not inevitable, but were the result of the exercise of political will by elites who mobilized their strength and defeated opponents.

Similarly, "transnationalism," "multiculturalism," and "global governance," like "diversity," are ideological tools championed by activist elites, not "forces of history." The success or failure of these values-loaded concepts will ultimately depend upon the political will and effectiveness of these elites.

Facing popular resistance on issue after issue, a wide range of American NGOs seek to bypass the normal democratic process to achieve their political ends by extra- or post-constitutional means, demanding that the United States:

- join the International Criminal Court;
- ratify the UN Convention on Women's Rights;
- drop reservations to the UN treaty against racial discrimination;
- reduce border policing;
- implement affirmative action legislation;
- follow international norms on capital punishment;
- accept the Kyoto Treaty on global warming;
- expand the legal rights of non-citizens in constitutional regimes.

HUMAN RIGHTS ACTIVISTS

A good part of the energy for transnational progressivism is provided by human rights activists, who consistently evoke "evolving norms of international law" in pursuing their goals. The main legal conflict between traditional American liberal democrats and transnational progressives is ultimately the question of whether the U.S. Constitution trumps international law or vice versa. "International law" here refers to what experts including John Bolton, Jeremy Rabkin, Jack Goldsmith, Lee Casey, and David Rivkin have called the "new international law," which differs from traditional concepts of the "Law of Nations."[22]

Before the mid-twentieth century, traditional international law usually referred to relations among nation-states: it was "international" in the real sense of the term. Since that time the "new international law" has increasingly penetrated the sovereignty of democratic nation-states. It is, therefore, in reality, "transnational law." Human rights activists work to establish norms for this "new international (i.e. transnational) law," and then attempt to bring the United States into conformity with a legal regime whose reach often extends beyond democratic politics and the guarantees of the U.S. Constitution.

Transnational progressives (including American and non-American NGOs and UN officials) excoriate American political, legal, and administrative practices in virulent language, as if the American liberal democratic nation-state was an illegitimate authoritarian regime. Thus, AI-U.S.A. charged the United States in a 1998 report with "a persistent and widespread pattern of human rights violations," stating that "racism and discrimination contribute to the denial of the fundamental rights of countless men, women, and children" in the United States. Moreover, police brutality is "entrenched and nation-wide"; the United States is the "world leader in high tech repression"; and it is time for the United States to face up to its "hypocrisy." The report discussed "a national background of economic and racial injustice, a rising tide of anti-immigrant sentiments" and stated that "human rights violations in the U.S. occur in rural communities and urban communities from coast to coast." The United States had long "abdicated its duty" to lead the world in promoting human rights.[23] Therefore, avowed William Schultz, the executive director of AI-U.S.A., "it was no wonder the United States was ousted from the [UN] Human Rights Commission."[24]

While AI-U.S.A. called on the UN to condemn "institutionalized cruelty" in the United States, HRW issued a 450-page report excoriating all types of "human rights violations." For example, HRW declared that "criminal justice polices" display a "disproportionate impact on African-Americans. . . . Although they comprised about 12 percent of the national adult population, they comprised 49.9 percent of the prison population." Overall, HRW affirmed that the United States was guilty of "serious human rights violations" including "rampant" police brutality and "harassment of gay adults in the military paralleled by the harassment of students perceived to be gay, lesbian, bisexual, and transgendered" in public schools. These students "experienced" school "as a place that accepted intolerance, hatred, ostracization, and violence against youth who were perceived as different." HRW also attacked the "curtailment of internationally-recognized rights" for (illegal) immigrants and complained that "the U.S. Border Patrol continued to grow at an alarming pace, doubling since 1993, when there were roughly 4,000 agents, to....approximately 8,000 agents."[25]

UN special investigators examined U.S. "human rights violations" in 1990s. The first thing these investigators did was meet with an array of American NGOs. In their reports, the UN officials quoted freely from American NGO documents. UN investigator Maurice Glélé of Benin wrote that, "racism existed in the U.S. with sociological inertia, structural obstacles, and individual resistance." Glélé visited the U.S. State Department and found that discrimination complaints by African American State Department employees "had dragged on since 1986." Meanwhile, the report stated, the "State Department remains a very white institution." The UN investigator further wrote that "the fate of the majority of Blacks is one of poverty, sickness, illiteracy, drugs, and crime in response to the social cul-de-sac in which they find themselves." Rahhika Coomaraswamy of Sri Lanka, the UN Special Rapporteur on Violence Against Women found that the United States is "criminalizing" a large segment of its population, a group that is "composed of poor persons of color and increasingly female."[26]

Bacre Waly Ndiaye, UN Special Rapporteur on Extrajudical, Summary, or Arbitrary Executions, like other UN investigators, consulted representatives of American NGOs including the ACLU, American Friends Service Committee, AI-U.S.A., the NAACP Legal Defense Fund, HRW, and the International Human Rights Law Group. Ndiaye's report found "a significant degree of unfairness and arbitrariness" in the application of the death penalty,"[27] based on racial data showing that 41 percent of death penalty inmates are African-American, 47 percent white, 7 percent Hispanic, and 1.5 percent American Indian.

ANTI-ASSIMILATION ON THE HOME FRONT

As noted earlier, the 2001 UN Conference Against Racism and Xenophobia held in Durban represents a classic case study of how American NGOs promote transnational progressivism. It is revealing that the language of almost all the UN treaties that ignore the guarantees of the U.S. Constitution (including the International Criminal Court (ICC), the Convention on Women's Rights, the Convention on Children's Rights) were written by American and other Western NGOs. In other words, the documents were written by a Western postnational intelligentsia aided by a "Westernistic" or "Westernized" coterie of Third World intellectuals (e.g., Nobel laureate Kofi Annan.)

It is significant, but little noticed, that many of same NGOs (HRW, AI-U.S.A.) and international law professors who have advocated transnational legal concepts at UN meetings and in international forums are active in U.S. immigration and naturalization law. On this front the transnational progressives have pursued two objectives: (1) eliminating all distinctions between citizens and non-citizens and (2) vigorously opposing attempts to assimilate immigrants into the "dominant" Anglo culture.

Thus, when discussing immigration/assimilation issues, Louis Henkin, one of the most prominent scholars of international law, attacks "archaic notions of sovereignty" and calls for largely eliminating "the difference between a citizen and a non-citizen permanent resident" in all federal laws.[28] Washington University international law professor Stephen Legomsky argues that dual nationals (who are American citizens) should not be required to give "greater weight to U.S. interests, in the event of a conflict" between the United States and the other country in which the American citizen is also a national.[29]

Two leading law professors (Peter Spiro from Hofstra, who has written extensively in support of NGOs, and Peter Schuck from Yale) question the requirement that immigrants seeking American citizenship "renounce 'all allegiance and fidelity' to their old nations." In an op-ed in the *Wall Street Journal*, they suggested dropping this "renunciation clause" from the Oath of Renunciation and Allegiance. They also question the concept of the hyphenated American, offering the model of "ampersand" American.[30] Thus, instead of thinking of traditional Mexican-Americans who are loyal citizens but proud of his ethnic roots, they do not object to immigrants (or migrants) who are both "Mexican and American," who retain "loyalties" to their "original homeland" and vote in both countries.

University Professor Robert Bach authored a major Ford Foundation report on new and "established residents" (the word "citizen" was assiduously avoided) that advocated the "maintenance" of ethnic immigrant identities, supported "non-citizen voting," and attacked assimilation (suggesting that homogeneity, not diversity, "may" be the "problem in America").[31] Bach later left the Ford

Foundation and became deputy director for policy at the INS in the Clinton administration, where he joined forces with then INS general counsel Alexander Alienikoff to promote a pro-multicultural, anti-assimilation federal policy. Alienikoff, a former (and current) immigration law professor, has openly and vigorously advocated a "politics" that "moves us beyond assimilation."[32]

It is well established (through Congressional investigations and investigative reporting) that the financial backing for this anti-assimilationist campaign has come primarily from the Ford Foundation, which in the 1970s made a conscious decision to fund a Latino rights movement based on advocacy-litigation and group rights.[33] On this front, the global progressives have been aided- if not always consciously, certainly in objective terms-by a "transnational right." It was a determined group of transnational and libertarian-leaning conservative senators and congressmen that prevented the Immigration Reform legislation of 1996 from limiting unskilled immigration.

The same group worked with progressives in the late 1990s to successfully block the implementation of a computerized plan to track the movement of foreign nationals in and out of the United States; thereby, in George Will's apt phrase putting "commerce over country." Whatever their ideological, commercial, or political motives, the constant demand for "open borders" and "free movement of people" (not simply free trade, which is a different matter all together) by certain editorialists, commentators, lobbyists, and activists on the libertarian and transnational right has strengthened the anti-assimilationist agenda of the global progressives.

The EU as a Stronghold of Transnational Progressivism

Whereas ideologically driven NGOs represent a subnational challenge to the values and policies of the liberal-democratic nation-state, the EU is a large supranational macro-organization that to a considerable extent embodies transnational progressivism, both in governmental form and in substantive policies. The governmental structure of the EU is post-democratic. Technically power in the EU resides in three bodies: the Council of the EU composed of one cabinet-level representative from each of the member-states; the European Parliament elected by citizens in the member-states; and the European Commission (EC), the EU's executive body.

As Washington lawyers, Lee Casey and David Rivkin have noted, "In theory, the European Commission is accountable to both the council and European Parliament. However, neither the council nor the European Parliament initiate policymaking. Their power is mostly a negative one, the ability to withhold approval of policies formulated and adopted by the European Commission, and even this checking function is exercised infrequently." Thus, Casey and Rivkin state, "Without doubt, the European Commission is the most powerful EU institution" and "the true source of its policy and legislative initiatives." Besides initiating legislation, the EC implements common policy and controls a large bureaucracy. It is composed of a rotating presidency and nineteen commissioners chosen by the member-states and approved by the European Parliament. It is unelected and, for the most part, unaccountable.

A white paper issued by the EC suggests that this unaccountability is one reason for its success: "The original and essential source of the success of European integration is that the EU's executive body, the Commission, is supranational and independent from national, sectoral, or other influences." This recognizable "democracy deficit" represents a moral challenge to EU legitimacy.[34]

The substantive polices advanced by EU leaders both in the Commission and the ECJ are based on the global progressive ideology of group rights discussed earlier that promotes victim groups over "privileged" groups and eschews the liberal principle of treating citizens equally as individuals. Thus, statutes on "hate speech," "hate crimes," "comparable worth" for women's pay, and group preferences are considerably more "progressive" in the EU than in the United States. At the same time, European courts have overruled national parliaments and public opinion in nation-states by compelling the British to incorporate gays and the Germans to incorporate women in combat units in their respective military services.

A group of what Undersecretary of State John Bolton has referred to as "Americanist" (as opposed to "Globalist") thinkers has emphasized the divergence of America's liberal philosophy from the EU's. In the June/July 2001 Policy Review, Lee Casey and David Rivkin, argued this position forcefully:

> From the perspective of U.S. philosophical and constitutional traditions, the key question in determining whether any particular model of government is a democracy is whether the governed choose their governors....Unfortunately, the reemergence [in Europe] of a pre-Enlightenment pan-European ideology that denies the ultimate authority of the nation-state, as well as the transfer of policymaking authority

from the governed and their elected representatives to a professional bureaucracy, as is evident in the EU's leading institutions, suggests a dramatic divergence from the basic principle of popular sovereignty once shared both by Europe's democracies and the United States.

In the world of practical international politics, in the period immediately prior to the events of September 11, the EU clearly stood in opposition to the United States on some of the most important strategic global issues, including the ICC, the Comprehensive Test Ban Treaty, the Land Mine Treaty, the Kyoto Global Warming Treaty, and policy towards missile defense, Iran, Iraq, Israel, China, Cuba, North Korea, and the death penalty. On most of these issues, transnational progressives in the United States-including many practicing politicians-supported the EU position and attempted to leverage this transnational influence in the domestic debate. At the same, the position of the Bush administration on many of these issues has support from elements in Europe, certainly from members of the British political class and public, and undoubtedly from some segments of the Continental European populace as well (on the death penalty, for example).

Even since the September 11 attacks, many Europeans have continued to snipe at American policies and place themselves in opposition to American interests in the war on terrorism. Within a month of September 11, Spanish judge Baltasar Garzon called the planned military tribunals "simply illegal."[35] In December 2001 the European Parliament condemned the U.S. Patriot Act (the bipartisan antiterrorist legislation that passed the U.S. Congress overwhelmingly) as "contrary to the principles" of human rights because the legislation "discriminates" against noncitizens.[36] Time and again, leading European politicians have made a point of insisting that they oppose extraditing terrorist suspects to the United States if those terrorists would be subjected to the death penalty.

Interestingly, both conservative realists and neoconservative pro-democracy advocates have argued that some EU, UN, and NGO thinking threatens to limit both American democracy at home and American power overseas. As Jeanne Kirkpatrick puts it, "foreign governments and their leaders, and more than a few activists here at home, seek to constrain and control American power by means of elaborate multilateral processes, global arrangements, and UN treaties that limit both our capacity to govern ourselves and act abroad."[37]

CONCLUSION

Scholars, publicists, and many others in the Western world-and especially in the United States, original home of constitutional democracy-have for the past several decades been arguing furiously over the most fundamental political ideas. Talk of a "culture war," however, is somewhat misleading, because the arguments over transnational vs. national citizenship, multiculturalism vs. assimilation, and global governance vs. national sovereignty are not simply cultural, but ideological and philosophical, in that they pose such Aristotelian questions as "What kind of government is best?" and "What is citizenship?"

In America, there is an elemental argument about whether to preserve, improve, and transmit the American regime to future generations or to transform it into a new and different type of polity. In the terms of contemporary political science we are arguing about "regime maintenance" vs. "regime transformation."

In the final analysis, the challenge from transnational progressivism to traditional American concepts of citizenship, patriotism, assimilation, and at the most basic level, to the meaning of democracy itself, is fundamental. It is a challenge to American liberal democracy. If our system is based not on individual rights, but on group consciousness; not on equality of citizenship, but on group preferences for non-citizens (including illegal immigrants) and for certain categories of citizens; not on majority rule within constitutional limits, but on power-sharing by different ethnic, racial, gender, and linguistic groups; not on constitutional law, but on transnational law; not on immigrants becoming Americans, but on migrants linked between transnational communities; then the regime will cease to be "constitutional," "liberal," "democratic," and "American," in the understood sense of those terms, but will become in reality a new hybrid system that is "post-constitutional," "post-liberal," "post-democratic," and "post-American."

This intracivilizational Western conflict between liberal democracy and transnational progressivism began in the mid to late twentieth century; it accelerated after the Cold War and should continue well into the twenty-first century. Indeed, from the fall of the Berlin Wall in November 1989 until the attacks on the heart of the American republic on September 11, 2001, the transnational progressives were on the offensive.

Since September 11, however, the forces supporting the liberal-democratic nation state have rallied. Clearly, in the post-Sept. 11

milieu there is a window of opportunity for those who favor a reaffirmation of the traditional norms of liberal-democratic patriotism. The political will to seize this opportunity is unclear. Key areas to watch include official government policy statements for the use of force and the conduct of war; the use and non-use of international law; assimilation-immigration policy; border control; civic education in the public schools; and the state of the patriotic narrative in popular culture.

FOURTH DIMENSION?

I suggest that we add a fourth dimension to a conceptual framework of international politics. Three dimensions are currently recognizable. First, there is traditional realpolitik, the competition and conflict among nation-states (and supranational states such as the EU). Second is the competition of civilizations conceptualized by Samuel Huntington.[38] Third, there is the conflict between the democratic world and the undemocratic world. I am suggesting a fourth dimension, the conflict within the democratic zone (and particularly within the West) between the forces of liberal democracy and the forces of transnational progressivism, between democrats and post-democrats.

At one level, the fourth dimension amounts to a struggle between the American/Anglo-American and the continental European models of governance-of what Western civilization ought to be. The latter travels the road to a form of bureaucratic collectivism, the former emphasizes the sometimes conflicting values of civic republicanism and the liberal values of openness and individuality within a market-driven milieu. As John O'Sullivan and others have pointed out, there are Europeans who support an entrepreneurial, liberal, Anglo-American style regime, and there are many Americans (particularly among elites) who favor a more collectivist continental European approach.[39]

The conflicts and tensions within each of these four dimensions of international politics are unfolding simultaneously and affected by each other, and so they all belong in a comprehensive understanding of the world of the twenty-first century. In hindsight, Fukuyama may have been wrong to suggest that liberal democracy is inevitably the final form of political governance, the evolutionary endpoint of political philosophy, because it has become unclear that liberal democracy can withstand its present internal challenges. Despite military and ideological triumphs over national socialism and communism, powerful antidemocratic forces that were in a sense Western ideological heresies, Western liberal democracy will continue to face an ideological-metaphysical challenge from powerful post-liberal democratic forces, whose origins are Western, but, which could, in James Kurth's word, be described as "post-Western."

1. Anthony Goodman, *United Nations*, Reuters, Oct. 24, 2000.

2. Ibid.

3. NGO demands listed in "Report of the U.S. Leadership Meetings on the World Conference Against Racism," convened by Gay McDougall, International Human Rights Group, 2001.

4. Reuters, AP, *New York Times* August 6, 2001 by Karen Iley on Yahoo! News.

5. Ibid.

6. "The End of History?" *National Interest*, Summer 1989.

7. Francis Fukuyama, "History Is Still Going Our Way," *Wall Street Journal*, Oct. 5, 2001.

8. Thomas Sowell, *The Quest for Cosmic Justice* (Free Press, 1999).

9. John Leo, "Long on Diversity Division," *Washington Times*, May 21, 1998.

10. In Jorge Amselle, "Reverse Imperialism," *National Review*, Oct. 12, 1998.

11. Alexander Alienikoff, "Citizens, Aliens, Membership and the Constitution," *Constitutional Commentary* 7, 1990, p. 30.

12. James Banks, "Transforming the Mainstream Curriculum," *Educational Leadership*, May 1994, p. 4.

13. Philip Johnston, "Straw Wants to Rewrite Our History, *Electronic Telegraph*, Oct. 10, 2000.

14. Quotes from Tom Bethell, "The Cultural Wars in Israel," paper prepared for Institute for Advanced Strategic and Political Studies conference on "Israel: The Advanced Case of Western Afflictions," Washington, D.C., Dec. 15, 1997; David Remnick, "The Dreamer," *New Yorker* Jan. 7, 2002; and Yoram Hazony, "The End of Zionism?" Azure Summer 1996. On post-Zionism in general see Yoram Hazony, *The Jewish State: The Struggle for Israel's Soul* (Washington, D.C. and New York: New Republic/Basic Books, 2000).

15. Linda Bosniak, "Citizenship Denationalized," *Indiana Journal of Global Legal Studies*, Spring 2000, p. 508.

16. See T. Alexander Aleinikoff and Douglass Klusmeyer, ed, >*From Migrants to Citizens: Membership in a Changing World* (Washington, D.C.: Carnegie Endowment for International Peace, 200); and T. Alexander Aleinikoff and Douglas Klusmeyer, ed., *Citizenship Today: Global Perspectives and Practices* (Washington, D.C.: Carnegie Endowment for International Peace, 2001). 17. In Linda K. Kerber, "The Meaning of Citizenship," *Dissent*, Fall 1997, p.36.

18. Kevin Davey, "Left Renewal," *New Times* (UK), June 1999.

19. Anthony Giddens, *Beyond Left and Right: The Future of Radical Politics* (Stanford, Calif.: Stanford University Press, 1994), pp. 2, 14-19, 90–91.

20. See Martha Nussbaum, "Patriotism and Cosmopolitanism," *Boston Review*, Oct.-Nov. 1994.

21. Strobe Talbot, "The Birth of the Global Nation," *Time*, July 20, 1992, pp. 70–71.

22. See *Chicago Journal of International Law*, Fall 2000 issue devoted to "AEI Conference: Trends in Global Governance: Do They Threaten American Sovereignty?"

23. "Rights For All: Human Rights Concerns in the U.S.A." (Amnesty International, Oct. 1998).

24. "Amnesty Criticizes U.S. Record on Rights," *Washington Post*, May 31, 2001.

25. "World Report: United States 1999" (Human Rights Watch).

26. Rita Maran, "International Human Rights in the U.S.: A Critique," *Social Justice*, Spring 1999, pp. 61–63.

27. Ibid. p. 60.

28. Louis Henkin, "Immigration and the Constitution: A Clean Slate," *Virginia Journal of International Law*, Fall 1994, p. 337.

29. Peter H. Schuck, "Plural Citizenships," in *Immigration and Citizenship in the 21st Century*, edited Noah M. Pickus (Lanham, MD: Rowman and Littlefield, 1998), p. 179.

30. Peter H. Schuck and Peter J. Spiro, "Dual Citizens, Good Americans," *Wall Street Journal*, Mar. 18, 1998. See also, Peter H. Schuck, "Plural Citizenships," in *Immigration and Citizenship in the 21 st Century*, edited Noah M. Pickus (Lanham, MD: Rowman and Littlefield, 1998), pp. 149-191.

31. See "Changing Relations, Newcomers and Established Residents in U.S. Communities: A Report to the Ford Foundation by the National Board of the Changing Relations Project," principal author Robert Bach, published by the Ford Foundation, New York, April 1993.

32. T. Alexander Alienikoff, "A Multicultural Nationalism?" *American Prospect*, Jan.-Feb. 1998, p. 84.

33. Georgie Anne Geyer, *Americans No More: The Death of Citizenship* (New York: The Atlantic Monthly Press, 1996), pp. 190–230.

34. See "European Governance," white paper, Commission of the European Communities, Brussels, July 25, 2001, an earlier version of which is described by Lee A. Casey and David B. Rivkin, Jr. in "Europe in the Balance: The Alarmingly Undemocratic Drift of the European Union," *Policy Review*, June/July 2001, pp. 41-53.

35. James Taranto, "No Justice, No Peace: Why It's Fatuous to Regard Sept. 11 as a 'Crime,'" *Opinion Journal*, Oct. 8, 2001.

36. "Welcome to Europe, Mr. Ashcroft," *OpinionJournal*, Dec. 14, 2001.

37. In "American Power for What? A Symposium," *Commentary*, Jan. 2000.

38. Samuel Huntington, *The Clash of Civilization and the Remaking of World Order* (Touchstone 1998).

39. *Chicago Journal of International Law*, Fall 2000 issue on "AEI Conference: Trends in Global Governance."

International Baccalaureate

By Allen Quist

The International Baccalaureate (IB) program was started in the mid 1960s by European diplomats who wanted their children to have an undergraduate program that would enable them to attend college anywhere in the world. International Baccalaureate is run by a non-governmental organization called the International Baccalaureate Organization (IBO). In 1996, UNESCO formed a "partnership" with IBO to form what it called a universal "curriculum framework for peace education." [*The Washington Times*, January 18, 2004]

International Baccalaureate has been adopted by 1,450 schools worldwide, 502 of them being in the United States. IB requires that the tests administered under the program be sent to the IB headquarters in Geneva, Switzerland, for grading. The U.S. Department of Education recently awarded a $1.2 million grant program for middle schools that are willing to participate in IB and become feeder schools for IB high schools. [*Ibid.*]

The Washington Times reported that IB is a pilot program by UNESCO for the purpose of creating what UNESCO calls an "international education system." The purpose of IB, said UNESCO, is to "… be a school of values, attitudes, [and] above all of practical action…[*Ibid.*]

The IB website states that the IB curriculum is based on six themes. These six themes are as follows:

[1] Who we are
[2] Where we are in place and time
[3] How we express ourselves
[4] How the world works
[5] How we organize ourselves
[6] Sharing the planet

These six themes focus on attitudes, values and behavior, just as UNESCO has said. The themes taken together constitute the teaching of a worldview—an overall philosophy of life. According to UNESCO, this worldview includes the promotion of sustainable development as defined by The Earth Charter* (see Chapter 7 of this book), promotion of the Universal Declaration of Human Rights** (see Chapter 14) and promotion of multiculturalism*** (see Chapter 5). [http://www.unesco.org/education/asp/studies.shtml] Because of the nonacademic focus of IB, many colleges and universities will not accept IB courses as fulfilling undergraduate requirements for admission. [*The Washington Times*, January 18, 2004]

America's Twelve Pillars of Freedom are obviously at odds with the IB curriculum and are not taught. IB is explicit in stating that it does not follow the political system of any particular nation, including the United States.

In summary, IB is a transformational system of education which exists to promote internationalism. It is structured to change the attitudes, values and behavior of its students to conform to the world government system. Dr. Ian Hill, Deputy Director of IBO, recently said that the goal of IBO is the promotion of "world citizenship." [http:/www.ibo.org]

*The Earth Charter is a broadly defined religious and political document that promotes the following positions:

1. Earth worship (pantheism).
2. Socialized medicine.
3. World government.
4. Abortion on-demand.
5. Education for sustainability including spiritual education in New Age/pantheism.
6. Adoption of the gay rights agenda.
7. Elimination of the right to bear arms.

**The UN Universal Declaration of Human Rights ends with the words: "These rights and freedoms may in no case be exercised contrary to the purposes and principles of the United Nations." That is, the UN Declaration of Human Rights takes the same form as the constitutions of all Communist countries which say that governmental policies have higher standing than individual human rights. The U.S. Declaration of Independence, in contrast, states that human rights have a higher priority than government decisions.

***Multiculturalism:

1. Believes that all cultures are equal. It also intends that all groups have equal outcomes—on income levels, education test scores, use of natural resources, and the like.
2. Follows the Marxist worldview and portrays government as being a creation of the powerful used to keep themselves in control and used to exploit the weak and vulnerable.
3. Is postmodernist. It views knowledge as being a tool by which the powerful subdue the vulnerable. Even language and traditional academic disciplines such as mathematics are viewed as constructs by which the strong exploit the weak.
4. Views history as the study of "multiple perspectives" of history. Traditional history is to be deconstructed, and students are expected to construct their own history (under the guidance of IB instructors).
5. Sees morality, modesty, human rights and the family as being mere constructs. Believes that marriage is a creation of powerful males used to keep vulnerable females under subjection. Includes obscenity for the purpose of deconstructing student beliefs about modesty, morality and marriage.
6. Takes a negative view of individualism. Group identity and group rights are promoted instead. An emphasis on group projects and group grading is used to teach group identification and group consciousness.
7. Sees private property rights from a Marxist perspective.
8. Views Christianity as a construct used by the powerful to exploit the masses. Multiculturalism is opposed to Christianity.

Up From Multiculturalism

By David Horowitz

Like most of the destructive movements of the 20th century–socialism, fascism, nihilism–multiculturalism is an invention of well-fed intellectuals. It did not well up from the immigrant communities and ethnic ghettoes of America as an expression of their cultural aspirations or communal needs. In fact its primary sponsor and most effective agency has been the Ford Foundation, a ten billion dollar tax-dodge created to protect the fortune of America's leading industrial bigot. Henry Ford published the Protocols of the Elders of Zion as a public service in the '20s and influenced Adolf Hitler's anti-Semitic crusade, winning himself an Iron Cross in the process. After his death, his foundation passed into the control of the intellectual Left and its fellow-travelers, the bureaucratic mandarins and the parlor socialists of the monied elite.

Multiculturalism, as we know it, would also not have been possible without the catastrophe that has befallen our colleges and universities in the post-'60s era. I am referring here to the politicization of the academy and the debasement of the curriculum, the transformation of the liberal arts divisions of the academy into a crude indoctrination platform and recruiting center for the America-hating, crypto-Marxist left. This intellectual plague has been described bluntly by Harold Bloom as "Stalinism without Stalin. All of the traits of the Stalinists in the 1930s, "are being repeated...in the universities in the 1990s." I am going to make an emendation to Bloom's description a little later. The mentality is Stalinist, but it is the particular Stalinism of Antonio Gramsci that informs the multicultural fervor in the academy. As I will further demonstrate, the post-modern left owes more, intellectually, to Mussolini than to Marx.

But we need to pause, first, over the fact that multiculturalism would not have been possible without the Ford Foundation and its tax-avoiding largesse. When you think about it, the American system of higher education in its own environment is remarkably diverse. There are more than three thousand institutions of higher learning in this country, occupying a diverse cultural geography. There are public and private colleges, technical institutes and schools of the arts, land-grant schools and schools with denominational affiliations, and many others besides. It is almost inconceivable that all these institutions would adopt a single party line, and would do so within the space of a decade or two, as they have on the multi-cultural front—and on so many other fronts dear to the Left. How was this possible?

Well, it is possible if you have a pile of money larger than the discretionary spending of the federal government in these areas, and you are viewed as a benign force by the academic community itself. The power of the Rockefeller, Carnegie, and Ford Foundations, and their clones, to shape America's institutions of higher learning is by no means new. At the very beginning of the era of the modern university, for example, Andrew Carnegie decided that it would be a good idea to give college teachers pensions. A college president was pretty hard-pressed to refuse such a gift, if he wanted to retain the best faculty available. Accordingly, the Carnegie Foundation attached some conditions to its grants, and it is these conditions that served to define the entire educational era that followed.

The Carnegie Foundation began by announcing that only colleges, as defined by itself, would be eligible for the grants. The Foundation then defined a college as requiring so many hours of secondary school education (which are still known as Carnegie Units), as possessing an endowment of at least $500,000, as having at least eight departments, and with each department headed by a Ph.D. That was how the Ph.D. became the key to the academic kingdom. Never, of course, has there been a more conformity-creating credential. The Ph.D. means that university intellectuals are required to beg the approval of their betters for the decade that shapes their professional life. This credentialing system has been more effective than a Central Committee in creating ideological conformity in the ivory tower. The Carnegie Foundation also announced that it would not fund pension programs for denominational institutions. That was how Brown, Drake, Wesleyan and many other colleges gave up their denominational affiliations, and how the secularization of American higher learning began. As a congressional commission asked at the time: If a college will give up its religious affiliation for money, what will it not give up?

Since that time, the power of these elite foundations has only grown. A crucial flexing of their financial muscle, with ramifications for the present ideological directions of the university, came in the 1940s in response to the Second World War. At that time, America's spy agency, the OSS, developed a need for "area specialists" for its intelligence operations. It had no use for historians, political scientists, or economists as such. The department system that the Carnegie Foundation had created was not functional in creating intellectual specialists for military intelligence, which had more specific agendas than the "disinterested pursuit of knowledge" could service. It wanted specialists in the particular geographical areas and national units it had targeted for attention. For efficiency reasons it wanted these specialists to have an interdisciplinary approach to the targets in question, a demand that the university as then constituted could not fulfill.

The solution was to re-shape the university, and so the OSS turned to Rockefeller and later, when it became the CIA, to Ford. Grants were offered for the creation of "area studies" programs and area specialists. The Russian Institute at Columbia and the Asian Studies Center at Berkeley were prototypes of the new academic curriculum. Naturally there was powerful resistance from the conservative forces in the university, the departments, and the scholarly disciplines, which regarded this as an abusive intrusion into academic concerns and a debasement of their intellectual pursuits. But just as naturally the money provided by Rockefeller and then, during the Cold War, by Ford, overrode these objections and the new interdisciplinary area studies programs flourished in schools all over the country.

Like the spy chiefs of the Central Intelligence Agency, Marxists also favor the interdisciplinary approach. Marxism was never about "economics" but always about "political economy," a theoretical agenda embracing all aspects of society and culture in the service of mid-wifing a new human cosmos. That is because Marxism, and all species of post-modern radicalism, are totalitarian in their ontology, their epistemology, and their political agendas. Nothing escapes them. Like all gnostics, political radicals are confident that they possess the theoretical key that will unlock the mysteries of humanity and society. Of course, they don't believe in any immutabilities like human nature which, in the preposterous view now proposed in the university, is "socially constructed." Their agenda, like that of Lenin and Hitler, is to re-construct the world and to create the new men and new women who will inhabit it (and think just as they do). Such an enterprise requires an adolescent credulity, an amnesia towards the past, and an interdisciplinary approach.

That is why the radicals of the '60s, when their revolution in the streets came up empty, turned to a vulnerable, open, and essentially defenseless institution for a last act of desecration and conquest. That is why they began colonizing the university with spurious intellectual projects that looked a lot like the CIA area-studies programs. Soon there appeared black studies (now African American, of course), women's studies, queer studies, cultural studies, and even American studies, the closest clone of the CIA prototypes, targeted not on foreign adversaries, however, but on the indispensable, one might even say constitutive, enemy of the left-wing imagination–the U.S.A. itself.

What made the routine violations of academic norms, and the subversion of institutional traditions possible was millions upon millions of dollars of bribes in the form of grants, subsidies, and other awards to administrators, academics, and institutions by the Ford Foundation and its satellite donors. It is no exaggeration to say that without the financial intervention of the Ford Foundation there would be no African American studies, women's studies, or queer studies as we know them.

What is multiculturalism? Well, in the first place, as my partner Peter Collier has pointed out, it is two lies in one word, since it is neither multi- nor cultural. It is, instead, fundamentally political and, like Stalinism, allows only one party and one party line. Its bottom-line agenda is the deconstruction of the idea of American nationality, in the service of the mindless, destructive, never-ending radical assault on the capital of the democratic world. Because it is the capital of the democratic world. Multiculturalism is the team banner of the hate-America Left.

From its inception as a nation of immigrants 200-odd years ago, America has been the inclusive mulit-national, multi-ethnic society, unparalleled in all human history in its success in integrating diverse communities on the basis of an ideal of equality. This success has been predicated on an American culture (not a multiculture) that makes that integration possible and sustains that American idea.

Multiculturalism is a head-on challenge above all to the notion that there is an American culture, and, that this culture is superior to all other cultures in precisely the ambition to be inclusive and equal, and that, consequently, this culture is the very crucible of America's future and its multi-ethnic success.

Multiculturalism is the place the Left went to lick its wounds when the '60s was over, and to carry on its malevolent agendas. The question radicals faced at the time was: How to continue the war against the evil empire–America–now that socialism was indisputably bankrupt. You do it the Gramscian way–Antonio Gramsci being one of the many disreputable Communists (and not a few disreputable Nazis) who have been enshrined as intellectual icons by the academic Left. Gramsci's addition to Marxist theory was to suggest that by seizing control of the culture you could extend that control to the rest of the social order as well. Never mind that the notion that the ruling ideas may not be the ideas of the ruling class destroys the entire edifice of Marxist theory. Logic was never a strong point of the Left. The real beauty of Gramsci's strategy is that it lets you forget about economics (which you never understood anyway) and about the colossal failure, the pure evil of actual socialist achievements, while continuing your adolescent hatred for America and its immense good works.

If you need an academic rubric under which to carry out this nihilistic attack, try "critical"–as in critical legal studies, critical race theory, or critical theory as such. Marx and his friends in the Hegelian Left were, of course, the original "critical theorists," but the ones you want to especially model yourselves after are the critical theorists of the Frankfurt School–deracinated Marxists who fled to the America they hated when the Hitler radicals came to power. Much earlier than you, Adorno and co. had lost faith in the proletariat and the liberated future as well. But they also did not want to give up their totalist assault on the bourgeois culture that gave them freedom to spew their abuse, and that had saved their lives as well.

Along with this spiteful hatred, another socialist frisson of the multicultural movement is the post-modern view that everyone (except white people), and every culture (except Western culture) is equal, and deserves equal respect. The culture arrogantly called Western Civilization is exclusionary and has to go. Your canon has the imperialists, the guilty, and the white, while ours has the innocent, the oppressed, and the persons of color. You have Homer and Shakespeare, and we have Rigoberta Menchu. Alongside the less appetizing aspects of the academic nightmare the Left has created, its capacity for self-parody is almost endearing.

In locating the roots of multiculturalism, we have to take into account a second catastrophe, in addition to the one that has befallen the academy. This is the catastrophe of the Left itself. Over the last several decades, even as the star of the Left has ascended in the academic firmament, it has become obvious to most ordinary mortals that the intellectual tradition of the Left–the tradition that–currently embraces Marx and Foucault, Heidegger and Derrida, Angela Davis and Andrea Dworkin–of Frederic Jameson and Michael Lerner, is utterly, terminally, irredeemably bankrupt. Socialist economics, critical theory, and progressive loyalties have produced the worst atrocities, the most horrific suffering, the most crushing oppression, and the greatest misery in all human history. But not for a moment, in the nearly 10 years since the fall of the Berlin Wall, has the Left begun to face its failure, or confront its deeds, or figure out what happened to its impossible dreams. It has simply moved on to another trench in its permanent war against the West–the English and Comp Lit departments of American universities. And in the course of this move, it has degenerated from a Stalinist universalism to a neo-fascist tribalism, which is what multiculturalism is really about.

There is a historical precedent for this post-modern devolution. At the time of the First World War, it had also become apparent to socialists like Lenin and Mussolini that something was awry in their totalist perspectives. A funny thing had happened on the way to the war. The proletarian international was supposed to heed Marx's reminder that the workers of the world had no country and to unite in opposition to the inter-imperialist conflict. Instead, the socialist parties of Germany and France decided they had more to lose than their chains and voted to support their national bourgeoisies and the war budgets that made the conflict possible. The socialist idea had collapsed.

In response to this debacle of Marxist theory, the Left of course did not decide to do the honorable thing and pack up its bags and go home. It wanted to continue its own war against the capitalist democracies of the West. Two paths lay before it. Lenin decided that conspiratorial vanguards were necessary to make sure that next time the working classes behaved as they were supposed to–in conformity with socialist theory. Lenin created the Communist International to crack the whip of theory over the huddled proletarian masses. But the human components of this institution also stubbornly obeyed the dictates of reality rather than theory and, instead of acting as an international vanguard, quickly became an organization of frontier guards for the Soviet Union.

Mussolini chose the other course. He decided that the true revolutionary agency was not an international class without property, but the nation itself. Fascism, in fact, was a socialism of the People, spelled with a capital P, or, if you happened to live in Germany, with a V for Volk. This is the real intellectual heritage of today's post-modern, politically correct, and multicultural Left.

I quote the political scientist Stephen Holmes of the University of Chicago: "Every anti-liberal argument influential today, was vigorously advanced in the writings of European fascists [including the critique of] its atomistic individualism, its myth of the pre-social individual, its scanting of the organic, its indifference to community,..its belief in the primacy of rights, its flight from the political, its decision to give abstract procedures and rules priority over substantive values and commitments, and its hypocritical reliance on the sham of judicial neutrality."

Gene Veith has put it more directly: "Cultural determinism, the reduction of all social relationships to issues of sheer power; the idea that one's identity is centered in one's ethnicity or race; the rejection of the concept of the individual . . . all of these ideas are direct echoes of the fascist theorists of the 1930s."

Or, to put it even more directly, "identity politics"–the politics of radical feminism, queer revolution, and Afro-centrism–which is the basis of academic multiculturalism, is a form of intellectual fascism and, insofar as it has any politics, of political fascism as well.

This article is adapted from a speech delivered at the Seventh National Conference of the National Association of Scholars in New Orleans, December 12-14, 1997.

Reprinted with permission from David Horowitz and www.frontpagemag.com.

The Earth Charter

PREAMBLE

We stand at a critical moment in Earth's history, a time when humanity must choose its future. As the world becomes increasingly interdependent and fragile, the future at once holds great peril and great promise. To move forward we must recognize that in the midst of a magnificent diversity of cultures and life forms we are one human family and one Earth community with a common destiny. We must join together to bring forth a sustainable global society founded on respect for nature, universal human rights, economic justice, and a culture of peace. Towards this end, it is imperative that we, the peoples of Earth, declare our responsibility to one another, to the greater community of life, and to future generations.

Earth, Our Home
Humanity is part of a vast evolving universe. Earth, our home, is alive with a unique community of life. The forces of nature make existence a demanding and uncertain adventure, but Earth has provided the conditions essential to life's evolution. The resilience of the community of life and the well-being of humanity depend upon preserving a healthy biosphere with all its ecological systems, a rich variety of plants and animals, fertile soils, pure waters, and clean air. The global environment with its finite resources is a common concern of all peoples. The protection of Earth's vitality, diversity, and beauty is a sacred trust.

The Global Situation
The dominant patterns of production and consumption are causing environmental devastation, the depletion of resources, and a massive extinction of species. Communities are being undermined. The benefits of development are not shared equitably and the gap between rich

and poor is widening. Injustice, poverty, ignorance, and violent conflict are widespread and the cause of great suffering. An unprecedented rise in human population has overburdened ecological and social systems. The foundations of global security are threatened. These trends are perilous—but not inevitable.

The Challenges Ahead

The choice is ours: form a global partnership to care for Earth and one another or risk the destruction of ourselves and the diversity of life. Fundamental changes are needed in our values, institutions, and ways of living. We must realize that when basic needs have been met, human development is primarily about being more, not having more. We have the knowledge and technology to provide for all and to reduce our impacts on the environment. The emergence of a global civil society is creating new opportunities to build a democratic and humane world. Our environmental, economic, political, social, and spiritual challenges are interconnected, and together we can forge inclusive solutions.

Universal Responsibility

To realize these aspirations, we must decide to live with a sense of universal responsibility, identifying ourselves with the whole Earth community as well as our local communities. We are at once citizens of different nations and of one world in which the local and global are linked. Everyone shares responsibility for the present and future well-being of the human family and the larger living world. The spirit of human solidarity and kinship with all life is strengthened when we live with reverence for the mystery of being, gratitude for the gift of life, and humility regarding the human place in nature.

We urgently need a shared vision of basic values to provide an ethical foundation for the emerging world community. Therefore, together in hope we affirm the following interdependent principles for a sustainable way of life as a common standard by which the conduct of all individuals, organizations, businesses, governments, and transnational institutions is to be guided and assessed.

PRINCIPLES

I. Respect And Care For The Community Of Life

1. Respect Earth and life in all its diversity.
  a. Recognize that all beings are interdependent and every form of life has value regardless of its worth to human beings.

b. Affirm faith in the inherent dignity of all human beings and in the intellectual, artistic, ethical, and spiritual potential of humanity.

2. Care for the community of life with understanding, compassion, and love.

a. Accept that with the right to own, manage, and use natural resources comes the duty to prevent environmental harm and to protect the rights of people.

b. Affirm that with increased freedom, knowledge, and power comes increased responsibility to promote the common good.

3. Build democratic societies that are just, participatory, sustainable, and peaceful.

a. Ensure that communities at all levels guarantee human rights and fundamental freedoms and provide everyone an opportunity to realize his or her full potential.

b. Promote social and economic justice, enabling all to achieve a secure and meaningful livelihood that is ecologically responsible.

4. Secure Earth's bounty and beauty for present and future generations.

a. Recognize that the freedom of action of each generation is qualified by the needs of future generations.

b. Transmit to future generations values, traditions, and institutions that support the long-term flourishing of Earth's human and ecological communities.

In order to fulfill these four broad commitments, it is necessary to:

II. Ecological Integrity

5. Protect and restore the integrity of Earth's ecological systems, with special concern for biological diversity and the natural processes that sustain life.

a. Adopt at all levels sustainable development plans and regulations that make environmental conservation and rehabilitation integral to all development initiatives.

b. Establish and safeguard viable nature and biosphere reserves, including wild lands and marine areas, to protect Earth's life support systems, maintain biodiversity, and preserve our natural heritage.

c. Promote the recovery of endangered species and ecosystems.

d. Control and eradicate non-native or genetically modified organisms harmful to native species and the environment, and prevent introduction of such harmful organisms.

e. Manage the use of renewable resources such as water, soil, forest products, and marine life in ways that do not exceed rates of regeneration and that protect the health of ecosystems.

f. Manage the extraction and use of non-renewable resources such as minerals and fossil fuels in ways that minimize depletion and cause no serious environmental damage.

6. Prevent harm as the best method of environmental protection and, when knowledge is limited, apply a precautionary approach.

a. Take action to avoid the possibility of serious or irreversible environmental harm even when scientific knowledge is incomplete or inconclusive.

b. Place the burden of proof on those who argue that a proposed activity will not cause significant harm, and make the responsible parties liable for environmental harm.

c. Ensure that decision making addresses the cumulative, long-term, indirect, long distance, and global consequences of human activities.

d. Prevent pollution of any part of the environment and allow no build-up of radioactive, toxic, or other hazardous substances.

e. Avoid military activities damaging to the environment.

7. Adopt patterns of production, consumption, and reproduction that safeguard Earth's regenerative capacities, human rights, and community well-being.

a. Reduce, reuse, and recycle the materials used in production and consumption systems, and ensure that residual waste can be assimilated by ecological systems.

b. Act with restraint and efficiency when using energy, and rely increasingly on renewable energy sources such as solar and wind.

c. Promote the development, adoption, and equitable transfer of environmentally sound technologies.

d. Internalize the full environmental and social costs of goods and services in the selling price, and enable consumers to identify products that meet the highest social and environmental standards.

e. Ensure universal access to health care that fosters reproductive health and responsible reproduction.

f. Adopt lifestyles that emphasize the quality of life and material sufficiency in a finite world.

8. Advance the study of ecological sustainability and promote the open exchange and wide application of the knowledge acquired.

    a. Support international scientific and technical cooperation on sustainability, with special attention to the needs of developing nations.

    b. Recognize and preserve the traditional knowledge and spiritual wisdom in all cultures that contribute to environmental protection and human well-being.

    c. Ensure that information of vital importance to human health and environmental protection, including genetic information, remains available in the public domain.

III. Social And Economic Justice

9. Eradicate poverty as an ethical, social, and environmental imperative.

    a. Guarantee the right to potable water, clean air, food security, uncontaminated soil, shelter, and safe sanitation, allocating the national and international resources required.

    b. Empower every human being with the education and resources to secure a sustainable livelihood, and provide social security and safety nets for those who are unable to support themselves.

    c. Recognize the ignored, protect the vulnerable, serve those who suffer, and enable them to develop their capacities and to pursue their aspirations.

10. Ensure that economic activities and institutions at all levels promote human development in an equitable and sustainable manner.

    a. Promote the equitable distribution of wealth within nations and among nations.

    b. Enhance the intellectual, financial, technical, and social resources of developing nations, and relieve them of onerous international debt.

    c. Ensure that all trade supports sustainable resource use, environmental protection, and progressive labor standards.

    d. Require multinational corporations and international financial organizations to act transparently in the public good, and hold them accountable for the consequences of their activities.

11. Affirm gender equality and equity as prerequisites to sustainable development and ensure universal access to education, health care, and economic opportunity.

    a. Secure the human rights of women and girls and end all violence against them.

    b. Promote the active participation of women in all aspects of economic, political, civil, social, and cultural life as full and equal partners, decision makers, leaders, and beneficiaries.

    c. Strengthen families and ensure the safety and loving nurture of all family members.

12. Uphold the right of all, without discrimination, to a natural and social environment supportive of human dignity, bodily health, and spiritual well-being, with special attention to the rights of indigenous peoples and minorities.

    a. Eliminate discrimination in all its forms, such as that based on race, color, sex, sexual orientation, religion, language, and national, ethnic or social origin.

    b. Affirm the right of indigenous peoples to their spirituality, knowledge, lands and resources and to their related practice of sustainable livelihoods.

    c. Honor and support the young people of our communities, enabling them to fulfill their essential role in creating sustainable societies.

    d. Protect and restore outstanding places of cultural and spiritual significance.

IV. Democracy, Nonviolence, And Peace

13. Strengthen democratic institutions at all levels, and provide transparency and accountability in governance, inclusive participation in decision making, and access to justice.

    a. Uphold the right of everyone to receive clear and timely information on environmental matters and all development plans and activities which are likely to affect them or in which they have an interest.

    b. Support local, regional and global civil society, and promote the meaningful participation of all interested individuals and organizations in decision making.

    c. Protect the rights to freedom of opinion, expression, peaceful assembly, association, and dissent.

    d. Institute effective and efficient access to administrative and independent judicial procedures, including remedies and redress for environmental harm and the threat of such harm.

    e. Eliminate corruption in all public and private institutions.

    f. Strengthen local communities, enabling them to care for their environments, and assign environmental responsibilities to the levels of government where they can be carried out most effectively.

14. Integrate into formal education and life-long learning the knowledge, values, and skills needed for a sustainable way of life.

    a. Provide all, especially children and youth, with educational opportunities that empower them to contribute actively to sustainable development.

    b. Promote the contribution of the arts and humanities as well as the sciences in sustainability education.

    c. Enhance the role of the mass media in raising awareness of ecological and social challenges.

    d. Recognize the importance of moral and spiritual education for sustainable living.

15. Treat all living beings with respect and consideration.

    a. Prevent cruelty to animals kept in human societies and protect them from suffering.

    b. Protect wild animals from methods of hunting, trapping, and fishing that cause extreme, prolonged, or avoidable suffering.

    c. Avoid or eliminate to the full extent possible the taking or destruction of non-targeted species.

16. Promote a culture of tolerance, nonviolence, and peace.

    a. Encourage and support mutual understanding, solidarity, and cooperation among all peoples and within and among nations.

    b. Implement comprehensive strategies to prevent violent conflict and use collaborative problem solving to manage and resolve environmental conflicts and other disputes.

    d. Demilitarize national security systems to the level of a non-provocative defense posture, and convert military resources to peaceful purposes, including ecological restoration.

    e. Eliminate nuclear, biological, and toxic weapons and other weapons of mass destruction.

f. Ensure that the use of orbital and outer space supports environmental protection and peace.

g. Recognize that peace is the wholeness created by right relationships with oneself, other persons, other cultures, other life, Earth, and the larger whole of which all are a part.

THE WAY FORWARD

As never before in history, common destiny beckons us to seek a new beginning. Such renewal is the promise of these Earth Charter principles. To fulfill this promise, we must commit ourselves to adopt and promote the values and objectives of the Charter.

This requires a change of mind and heart. It requires a new sense of global interdependence and universal responsibility. We must imaginatively develop and apply the vision of a sustainable way of life locally, nationally, regionally, and globally. Our cultural diversity is a precious heritage and different cultures will find their own distinctive ways to realize the vision. We must deepen and expand the global dialogue that generated the Earth Charter, for we have much to learn from the ongoing collaborative search for truth and wisdom.

Life often involves tensions between important values. This can mean difficult choices. However, we must find ways to harmonize diversity with unity, the exercise of freedom with the common good, short-term objectives with long-term goals. Every individual, family, organization, and community has a vital role to play. The arts, sciences, religions, educational institutions, media, businesses, nongovernmental organizations, and governments are all called to offer creative leadership. The partnership of government, civil society, and business is essential for effective governance.

In order to build a sustainable global community, the nations of the world must renew their commitment to the United Nations, fulfill their obligations under existing international agreements, and support the implementation of Earth Charter principles with an international legally binding instrument on environment and development.

Let ours be a time remembered for the awakening of a new reverence for life, the firm resolve to achieve sustainability, the quickening of the struggle for justice and peace, and the joyful celebration of life.

Dakar Framework for Action

Education For All:
Meeting Our Collective Commitments
Text adopted by the World Education Forum,
Dakar, Senegal, 26-28 April 2000

1. Meeting in Dakar, Senegal, in April 2000, we, the participants in the World Education Forum, commit ourselves to the achievement of education for all (EFA) goals and targets for every citizen and for every society.

2. The Dakar Framework is a collective commitment to action. Governments have an obligation to ensure that EFA goals and targets are reached and sustained. This is a responsibility that will be met most effectively through broad-based partnerships within countries, supported by cooperation with regional and international agencies and institutions.

3. We re-affirm the vision of the World Declaration on Education for All (Jomtien 1990), supported by the Universal Declaration of Human Rights and the Convention on the Rights of the Child, that all children, young people and adults have the human right to benefit from an education that will meet their basic learning needs in the best and fullest sense of the term, an education that includes learning to know, to do, to live together and to be. It is an education geared to tapping each individual's talents and potential, and developing learners' personalities, so that they can improve their lives and transform their societies.

4. We welcome the commitments made by the international community to basic education throughout the 1990s, notably at the World Summit for Children (1990), the Conference on

Environment and Development (1992), the World Conference on Human Rights (1993), the World Conference on Special Needs Education: Access and Quality (1994), the International Conference on Population and Development (1994), the World Summit for Social Development (1995), the Fourth World Conference on Women (1995), the Mid-Term Meeting of the International Consultative Forum on Education for All (1996), the Fifth International Conference on Adult Education (1997), and the International Conference on Child Labour (1997). The challenge now is to deliver on these commitments.

5. The EFA 2000 Assessment demonstrates that there has been significant progress in many countries. But it is unacceptable in the year 2000 that more than 113 million children have no access to primary education, 880 million adults are illiterate, gender discrimination continues to permeate education systems, and the quality of learning and the acquisition of human values and skills fall far short of the aspirations and needs of individuals and societies. Youth and adults are denied access to the skills and knowledge necessary for gainful employment and full participation in their societies. Without accelerated progress towards education for all, national and internationally agreed targets for poverty reduction will be missed, and inequalities between countries and within societies will widen.

6. Education is a fundamental human right. It is the key to sustainable development and peace and stability within and among countries, and thus an indispensable means for effective participation in the societies and economies of the twenty-first century, which are affected by rapid globalization. Achieving EFA goals should be postponed no longer. The basic learning needs of all can and must be met as a matter of urgency.

7. We hereby collectively commit ourselves to the attainment of the following goals:

   (i) expanding and improving comprehensive early childhood care and education, especially for the most vulnerable and disadvantaged children;

   (ii) ensuring that by 2015 all children, particularly girls, children in difficult circumstances and those belonging to ethnic minorities, have access to and complete free and compulsory primary education of good quality;

   (iii) ensuring that the learning needs of all young people and adults are met through equitable access to appropriate learning and life skills programmes;

    (iv) achieving a 50 per cent improvement in levels of adult literacy by 2015, especially for women, and equitable access to basic and continuing education for all adults;

    (v) eliminating gender disparities in primary and secondary education by 2005, and achieving gender equality in education by 2015, with a focus on ensuring girls' full and equal access to and achievement in basic education of good quality;

    (vi) improving all aspects of the quality of education and ensuring excellence of all so that recognized and measurable learning outcomes are achieved by all, especially in literacy, numeracy and essential life skills.

8. To achieve these goals, we the governments, organizations, agencies, groups and associations represented at the World Education Forum pledge ourselves to:

    (i) mobilize strong national and international political commitment for education for all, develop national action plans and enhance significantly investment in basic education;

    (ii) promote EFA policies within a sustainable and well-integrated sector framework clearly linked to poverty elimination and development strategies;

    (iii) ensure the engagement and participation of civil society in the formulation, implementation and monitoring of strategies for educational development;

    (iv) develop responsive, participatory and accountable systems of educational governance and management;

    (v) meet the needs of education systems affected by conflict, national calamities and instability and conduct educational programmes in ways that promote mutual understanding, peace and tolerance, and help to prevent violence and conflict;

    (vi) implement integrated strategies for gender equality in education which recognize the need for changes in attitudes, values and practices;

    (vii) implement as a matter of urgency education programmes and actions to combat the HIV/AIDS pandemic;

    (viii) create safe, healthy, inclusive and equitably resourced educational environments conducive to excellence in learning with clearly defined levels of achievement for all;

    (ix) enhance the status, morale and professionalism of teachers;

    (x) harness new information and communication technologies to help achieve EFA goals;

(xi) systematically monitor progress towards EFA goals and strategies at the national, regional and international levels; and

(xii) build on existing mechanisms to accelerate progress towards education for all.

9. Drawing on the evidence accumulated during the national and regional EFA assessments, and building on existing national sector strategies, all States will be requested to develop or strengthen existing national plans of action by 2002 at the latest. These plans should be integrated into a wider poverty reduction and development framework, and should be developed through more transparent and democratic processes, involving stakeholders, especially peoples' representatives, community leaders, parents, learners, non-governmental organizations (NGOs) and civil society. The plans will address problems associated with the chronic under-financing of basic education by establishing budget priorities that reflect a commitment to achieving EFA goals and targets at the earliest possible date, and no later than 2015. They will also set out clear strategies for overcoming the special problems facing those currently excluded from educational opportunities, with a clear commitment to girls' education and gender equity. The plans will give substance and form to the goals and strategies set out in this Framework, and to the commitments made during a succession of international conferences in the 1990s. Regional activities to support national strategies will be based on strengthened regional and subregional organizations, networks and initiatives.

10. Political will and stronger national leadership are needed for the effective and successful implementation of national plans in each of the countries concerned. However, political will must be underpinned by resources. The international community acknowledges that many countries currently lack the resources to achieve education for all within an acceptable time-frame. New financial resources, preferably in the form of grants and concessional assistance, must therefore be mobilized by bilateral and multilateral funding agencies, including the World Bank and regional development banks, and the private sector. We affirm that no countries seriously committed to education for all will be thwarted in their achievement of this goal by a lack of resources.

11. The international community will deliver on this collective commitment by launching with immediate effect a global initiative aimed at developing the strategies and mobilizing the resources

needed to provide effective support to national efforts. Options to be considered under this initiative will include:

(i) increasing external finance for education, in particular basic education;

(ii) ensuring greater predictability in the flow of external assistance;

(iii) facilitating more effective donor coordination;

(iv) strengthening sector-wide approaches;

(v) providing earlier, more extensive and broader debt relief and/or debt cancellation for poverty reduction, with a strong commitment to basic education; and

(vi) undertaking more effective and regular monitoring of progress towards EFA goals and targets, including periodic assessments.

12. There is already evidence from many countries of what can be achieved through strong national strategies supported by effective development cooperation. Progress under these strategies could - and must - be accelerated through increased international support. At the same time, countries with less developed strategies - including countries in transition, countries affected by conflict, and post-crisis countries - must be given the support they need to achieve more rapid progress towards education for all.

13. We will strengthen accountable international and regional mechanisms to give clear expression to these commitments and to ensure that the Dakar Framework for Action is on the agenda of every international and regional organization, every national legislature and every local decision-making forum.

14. The EFA 2000 Assessment highlights that the challenge of education for all is greatest in sub-Saharan Africa, in South Asia, and in the least developed countries. Accordingly, while no country in need should be denied international assistance, priority should be given to these regions and countries. Countries in conflict or undergoing reconstruction should also be given special attention in building up their education systems to meet the needs of all learners.

15. Implementation of the preceding goals and strategies will require national, regional and international mechanisms to be galvanized immediately. To be most effective these mechanisms will be participatory and, wherever possible, build on what already exists. They will include representatives of all stakeholders and partners and they will operate in transparent and accountable ways. They

will respond comprehensively to the word and spirit of the Jomtien Declaration and this Dakar Framework for Action. The functions of these mechanisms will include, to varying degrees, advocacy, resource mobilization, monitoring, and EFA knowledge generation and sharing.

16. The heart of EFA activity lies at the country level. National EFA Forums will be strengthened or established to support the achievement of EFA. All relevant ministries and national civil society organizations will be systematically represented in these Forums. They should be transparent and democratic and should constitute a framework for implementation at subnational levels. Countries will prepare comprehensive National EFA Plans by 2002 at the latest. For those countries with significant challenges, such as complex crises or natural disasters, special technical support will be provided by the international community. Each National EFA Plan will:

(i) be developed by government leadership in direct and systematic consultation with national civil society;

(ii) attract co-ordinated support of all development partners;

(iii) specify reforms addressing the six EFA goals;

(iv) establish a sustainable financial framework;

(v) be time-bound and action-oriented;

(vi) include mid-term performance indicators; and

(vii) achieve a synergy of all human development efforts, through its inclusion within the national development planning framework and process.

17. Where these processes and a credible plan are in place, partner members of the international community undertake to work in a consistent, co-ordinated and coherent manner. Each partner will contribute according to its comparative advantage in support of the National EFA Plans to ensure that resource gaps are filled.

18. Regional activities to support national efforts will be based on existing regional and subregional organizations, networks and initiatives, augmented where necessary. Regions and subregions will decide on a lead EFA network that will become the Regional or Subregional Forum with an explicit EFA mandate. Systematic involvement of, and co-ordination with, all relevant civil society and other regional and subregional organizations are essential. These Regional and Subregional EFA Forums will be linked organically with, and be accountable to, National EFA Forums. Their functions will be: co-ordination with all relevant networks; setting and monitoring regional/subregional targets; advocacy;

policy dialogue; the promotion of partnerships and technical cooperation; the sharing of best practices and lessons learned; monitoring and reporting for accountability; and promoting resource mobilization. Regional and international support will be available to strengthen Regional and Subregional Forums and relevant EFA capacities, especially within Africa and South Asia.

19. UNESCO will continue its mandated role in co-ordinating EFA partners and maintaining their collaborative momentum. In line with this, UNESCO's Director-General will convene annually a high-level, small and flexible group. It will serve as a lever for political commitment and technical and financial resource mobilization. Informed by a monitoring report from the UNESCO International Institute for Educational Planning (IIEP), the UNESCO International Bureau of Education (IBE), the UNESCO Institute for Education (UIE) and, in particular, the UNESCO Institute of Statistics, and inputs from Regional and Subregional EFA Forums, it will also be an opportunity to hold the global community to account for commitments made in Dakar. It will be composed of highest-level leaders from governments and civil society of developing and developed countries, and from development agencies.

20. UNESCO will serve as the Secretariat. It will refocus its education programme in order to place the outcomes and priorities of Dakar at the heart of its work. This will involve working groups on each of the six goals adopted at Dakar. This Secretariat will work closely with other organizations and may include staff seconded from them.

21. Achieving Education for All will require additional financial support by countries and increased development assistance and debt relief for education by bilateral and multilateral donors, estimated to cost in the order of $8 billion a year. It is therefore essential that new, concrete financial commitments be made by national governments and also by bilateral and multilateral donors including the World Bank and the regional development banks, by civil society and by foundations.

28 April 2000 Dakar, Senegal

The Purpose of Government

By Allen Quist

The Declaration of Independence says that government has one primary purpose: protecting the unalienable, God-given rights that all human beings possess. The Declaration states:

> That, to secure these rights, Governments are instituted among Men. [The term "rights" had been defined earlier as follows: "... they are endowed by their Creator with certain unalienable Rights, that among these are Life, Liberty, and the pursuit of Happiness."]

In this way the Declaration of Independence makes it crystal clear that government has one overarching purpose: protecting the inherent human rights of life, liberty and property (pursuit of happiness).

Not all governments recognize this all-important principle. The Constitution of Cuba, for example, says: "Citizens have freedom of speech in keeping with the goals of the socialist society." The "good [or goals] of society" will always be defined by government, of course. For that reason, any government which says that the good of society is more important than human rights is free to suspend the basic human rights at any time that it wishes. Human rights cease to be genuine "rights" if they can be suspended by the government for any reason other than criminal activity.

Societies which recognize that inherent human rights have higher standing than government policies are free societies. Those countries, however, which hold that governmental policies have priority over human rights, are, by definition, totalitarian.

Take, for example, the right to vote. If a government eliminates the right to vote on the grounds that the good of society requires it (the only grounds ever used), that society ceases to be free. Similarly, if a government eliminates freedom of speech it has then positioned itself to eliminate all other rights, and that society has ceased to be free.

This principle—that the primary purpose of government is the protection of basic human rights—was recognized by our founding fathers as being so important that the Declaration of Independence added the following clarification:

> ...whenever government becomes destructive to these ends [protecting our unalienable Rights], it is the Right of the People to alter or abolish it and to institute new Government....

Our founding fathers knew what it meant to be free, and they were willing to clarify what freedom meant.

THE HISTORICAL REVISIONISM OF THE NEW CIVICS

Our Declaration of Independence and our founders were clear and emphatic that the first purpose of government is the protection of our inalienable human rights. In spite of this fact, however, the New Federal Curriculum takes a different, and radical, position. The *National Standards for Civics and Government* say:

> Explain that the purposes of government in the United States are to protect the rights of individuals and to promote the common good. [p. 17] [The national standards (Federal Curriculum) make this same point several other places.]

According to the national standards, government supposedly has two primary purposes, not just one. Now the common good has been elevated to a position equal to that of protection of the basic rights (also described as the "internationalist position on human rights").

Placing the common good and protection of the basic rights on the same level is like mixing oil and water. One or the other must rise to the top. Government cannot have two primary purposes. It can have only one. Government can, of course, have many secondary functions, but it can have only one primary function and guiding principle. As the Declaration of Independence so clearly states, the one guiding principle in the United States is the protection of our inalienable rights.

How does the *National Standards for Civics and Government* attempt to defend its false position? It does so by saying that protecting the basic human rights is stated in the Declaration of Independence, but promoting the common good is stated in the Preamble to the Constitution. This supposedly makes the two purposes equal.

This argument, however, has no merit. The Declaration is speaking of the overall purpose of government. The Preamble to the Constitution, in contrast, is speaking only of the reasons for adopting this Constitution. The purpose of a particular constitution is a lesser question than the purpose of government. A nation can have a government without having a constitution. It would not be wise, but it can be and is being done.

Specifically, the Preamble to our Constitution mentions six reasons for adopting the Constitution. Those six reasons are:

1. form a more perfect Union,
2. establish Justice,
3. insure domestic Tranquility,
4. provide for the common defense,
5. promote the general Welfare, and
6. secure the Blessings of Liberty to ourselves and our Posterity.

It is obvious from this list that the reasons given are those in favor of adopting this Constitution as opposed to a continuation of the Articles of Confederation. The preamble does not presume to be a statement of the overall purpose of government.

It should also be observed that if the Preamble to the Constitution actually did elevate the common good to the same level as protection of the unalienable rights, then it also elevates national defense and the other goals to the same level. No one seems to want to make that case, however, further illustrating the error in the position of the national standards.

What, then, is the actual relationship between the purpose of government as stated in the Constitution and the objectives stated in the Preamble to the Constitution? The relationship is this: Ask the question, how will we be successful in securing the God-given human rights described in the Declaration? The Preamble's answer is that we will do so by: (1) forming a more perfect union, (2) establishing justice, (3) insuring domestic tranquility, (4) providing for the common defense, and (5) promoting the general welfare. All these objectives, if accomplished, will then (6) "secure the Blessings of Liberty to ourselves and our Posterity."

Why, then, do the national standards promote a position that is so clearly fallacious (and anti-American)? The reason is that they wish to change our form of government, not teach it. (For a thorough description of these standards, see the author's book, *Fed Ed: The New Federal Curriculum and How It's Enforced*, available at edwatch.org or amazon.com.

How can Government
Promote the Common Good?

In the same year that the Declaration of Independence was adopted, Adam Smith published *The Wealth of Nations*. Smith argued that if business was allowed to be free ("free enterprise"), the result would be far greater prosperity. History has proven Smith to be correct. Free enterprise leads to prosperity; socialism, in contrast, leads to poverty.

This means that if the God-given rights of private property and free enterprise are respected, the consequence is that the common good is advanced as well. The same principle holds true for all the human rights. When government's highest calling is protection of the people's right to life, liberty and property, the result will be that the common good is significantly advanced.

It doesn't work in the reverse. When governments view the common good as being more important than individual rights, as does any totalitarian state, then both the basic human rights and the common good will suffer. The common good will suffer to the degree that the basic human rights are denied.

Limits on the Exercise
of the God-Given Rights.

Our nation has always recognized that the exercise of our inherent rights is limited by the fact that all other persons have the same inherent rights that we have. The Declaration of Independence prefaces its statement about unalienable rights by asserting that, "all men are created equal." The Founders knew that equality means that no one has the right to infringe on the rights of others. Does one citizen, for example, have the right to infringe upon the rights to life, liberty and property of another? Of course not. Our nation has always understood that "My rights end where your rights begin." Government, in turn, must treat equally the rights of all its citizens.

No one has the right to harm another human being. In addition, paragraph one of the Declaration of Independence recognizes Natural

Law—the universal principles of right and wrong—as being one of our foundational principles. Our Founders knew that no one has the right to do wrong. Understanding natural law prevents liberty from becoming license.

Suspending Human Rights in Time of National Emergency

Did the national emergency of World War II justify the imprisonment of Japanese Americans in concentration camps? No, it did not. This argument that national security or emergency requires the suspension of basic human rights should always be viewed with considerable suspicion.

At the same time, the military draft is not necessarily in conflict with our foundational principles. A national draft can only be justified, however, by being necessary to protect national sovereignty (the first stated principle in the Declaration of Independence), and in being necessary to protect the inherent human rights of life, liberty and property which are, in turn, protected by national sovereignty. This is the only way a military draft can be defended—that it is necessary to protect the inalienable rights of life, liberty and property.

Margaret Stimmann Branson's Description of the three Differing Views of Human Rights.

The analysis of Margaret Stimmann Branson is helpful and accurate. She said (in "RIGHTS: AN INTERNATIONAL PERSPECTIVE, an address to the first Plenary Session of the Center for Civic Education," Marina del Rey, California, June 21, 1991):

First let's look at the conception of rights on which the
U.S. Constitution is based....
Second, let's look at rights as they are conceived in the constitutions of the Communist world.
Finally, we'll focus briefly on American attitudes toward the Universal Declaration of Human Rights which attempts to combine the competing conceptions....

These are the three different views on the relationship between government's role in protecting the God-given rights versus promoting the common good. Stimmann Branson provided further clarification of each of the three views by saying:

I. THE AMERICAN CONCEPTION OF RIGHTS

Our [American] rights, however, derive from a source which antedates the Constitution. That source [is] identified clearly in the Declaration of Independence which opens with these well-known words: "We hold these truths to be self-evident, that all Men are created equal, that they are endowed by their Creator with certain unalienable Rights, that among these are Life, Liberty and the pursuit of Happiness. That, to secure these Rights, Governments are instituted among Men, deriving their just powers from the consent of the governed."

Americans have taken the reasoning embodied in the Declaration and confirmed by their constitutional compact to mean that each of them has rights which accrue to them simply because they are human beings. Those rights are individual...natural...inherent. They cannot be taken away or even suspended. Those rights are not a gift. They are not concessions wrung from a king or a parliament. Rather they are fundamental freedoms which supercede and are superior to governments. They do not derive from any constitution, they antecede all constitutions.

II. RIGHTS AS CONCEIVED IN THE CONSTITUTIONS OF THE COMMUNIST WORLD

Turning from the American conception of rights to that of the communist world...Marx also rejected the doctrine of natural rights on a variety of grounds...Marx identified individualism with egoism; the tendency to think in communal or collectivist terms he equated with altruism. Socialist society, therefore, should be altruistic, based on a philosophy of fulfilling human needs...[For example] the operant constitution of the Soviet Union...provides (Article 41):

"Citizens of the USSR have the right to work (and) the right to choose their trade or profession in accordance with their inclinations, abilities, training and education AND with due account of the needs of society..."

The importance of the concept of duties and responsibilities is such that lengthy sections are commonplace. These are some of the most frequently used labels for these: "Basic Rights and Duties of Citizens", "The Basic Rights, Freedoms and Obligations of Citizens," and "Fundamental Rights and Duties of Citizens."...

III. AMERICAN ATTITUDES TOWARD THE UNIVERSAL DECLARATION OF HUMAN RIGHTS

As you know, concern about rights is in the American tradition and at the core of the American creed. The government of the United States was founded on the assertion that the primary purpose of its government is to secure and protect the rights of individuals...Speaking for the United States government in an address to the United Nations [on the Universal Declaration of Human Rights], a ranking state department official [said]:

"We view human rights as limitations upon the power of the state. Based on principles set forth in the Bill of Rights of the United States Constitution, our...rights are timeless, unalterable, and not subject to the intellectual or political fashions of the day. They establish the state as the servant of the people and not the other way around...."

The official continued:

"The past 25 years have seen a tendency to redefine human rights [as in the Universal Declaration of Human Rights]...In contrast to our notion of human rights as limitations upon the power of the state, these 'rights' would augment the power of the state, make individuals more dependent, and could not be enforced by an independent judiciary."

In other words, Stimmann Branson observed that the federal government, under Presidents Reagan and Bush Sr., rejected the Universal Declaration of Human Rights because it is at odds with the American understanding of human rights as stated in our Declaration of Independence and Constitution. In the United States this principle is clear, that government has one primary purpose—protecting the God-given, inalienable rights of all its people.

In summary there are three different positions of the relationship between human rights and government. They are:

1. The view of the United States: Government exists for the primary purpose of protecting the inalienable rights of its citizens.
2. The Communist and/or totalitarian view: Government exists for the purpose of promoting the good of its citizens, as defined by the government.
3. The internationalist view: Government exists to protect human rights and to contribute to the common good, as defined by the government.

There is ultimately little difference between the second and third definitions.

Comments on
"Education for Democracy"

By Allen Quist

One of the features of the new approach to teaching civics and government is its focus on a transnational study of government. This approach goes by titles such as "Education for Democracy," "Essential Elements of Constitutional Democracy," and "Human Rights Education." The goal of this transnational study of government is to study the so-called universal principles of democracy and/or human rights, rather than focusing on the features of government in the United States.

There are several forms of "education for democracy" currently under discussion. I shall here evaluate the one called "Constitutional Democracy" which has been developed by the Center for Civic Education (CCE), the same NGO that wrote *The National Standards For Civics And Government*, and *We The People: The Citizen And The Constitution* (both funded by U.S. tax dollars). The CCE also conducts international education programs on Civics and Government, also partially funded by American taxpayers.

The entire article is available on the CCE website (http://civiced.org/constdem.html). The author's review of this CCE article follows.

Part I of the article is called, "Constitutional Democracy: An Outline of Essential Elements." Part I includes the following question and statements:

What are the essential characteristics and principles of Constitutional Democracy?

CONSTITUTIONAL DEMOCRACY is the antithesis of arbitrary rule. It is democracy characterized by:

A. POPULAR SOVEREIGNTY. The people are the ultimate source of authority of the government which derives its right to govern from their consent.

B. MAJORITY RULE AND MINORITY RIGHTS. Although "the majority rules," the fundamental rights of individuals in the minority are protected.

C. LIMITED GOVERNMENT. The powers of government are limited by law and a written or unwritten constitution which those in power obey.

D. LIMITATIONS OF POWERS. There are certain institutional and procedural devices which limit the powers of government....

AUTHOR'S COMMENTS:

In the following pages, the CCE article explains what it means by the four "Essential Elements" of democracy outlined above. These four characteristics listed are important elements of a democracy, but we must recognize that the four characteristics are stated in answer to the question: "What are the essential characteristics and principles of constitutional democracy?" Does this list of four items provide an adequate list of such "essential elements"? What is missing? Following is a list of important principles of democracy contained in the U.S. Declaration of Independence and Constitution, which are absent from the list of so called "essential elements" of democracy as defined by the Center for Civic Education (CCE):

1. National Sovereignty. National sovereignty is never mentioned in the CCE's description of "constitutional democracy." National sovereignty is out of sight and out of mind. The CCE's textbook, *We The People: The Citizen And The Constitution*, never mentions national sovereignty, either. In contrast to the position of the CCE, our Declaration of Independence begins with national sovereignty. If national sovereignty is not among the "essential elements" of a democracy, then the kind of democracy envisioned by the CCE must at least be open to disbanding national sovereignty and creating a world government. Democracy won't mean much in a world government system.

2. Natural law. Also missing is natural law, the second stated principle of freedom in the Declaration of Independence. Natural law—the universal principles of morality–is interconnected with unalienable rights, as the founders of our nation clearly understood. Why, for example, do all people have an inalienable right to life? The reason is that the right to life is part of the universal moral code which governs all human beings. Murder is morally wrong because people have an inalienable right to life. The law makes murder illegal. Natural law makes murder wrong. Our forefathers knew this truth; that is why they listed natural law in the Declaration of Independence as being fundamental to a free society. Our forefathers recognized that the God-given rights can only be protected if natural law is recognized and followed. They also knew that laws are just—only if they are based on the universal moral code.

3. Self-evident truths. Also absent from the CCE's definition of "essential characteristics" of democracy is the concept of "self-evident truths," listed as the third principle of freedom in our Declaration of Independence. Our founders knew that the nation was being constructed on foundational principles; they also recognized these principles to be truths. By avoiding the word "truth," the CCE is really saying that the foundational principles of the United States can be interpreted as mere constructs of culture which have no necessary connection to truth. Constructs can be changed at any time—hardly a basis for an enduring system of freedom.

4. Unalienable rights. The CCE speaks of human rights as being "fundamental" and "individual," but never as being "unalienable" or God-given as stated in our Declaration of Independence. If human rights are not unalienable, they at best are granted by government. Whatever government grants, government can withdraw. In other words, the rights that the CCE speak of are not rights in the real sense; they are mere concessions that government makes and that government can withhold at any time. So even though the paper later speaks of the rights of life, liberty and property, these rights are never pictured as unalienable. As a consequence human rights to the CCE are not genuine rights at all.

Later in the article, the principles of equality and popular sovereignty are promoted. This paper by the CCE advocates only two of the Twelve Pillars of Freedom described by the Declaration of Independence. Even these two pillars of freedom are at least open to being viewed as cultural constructs as opposed to being truths. The CCE's definition of "constitutional democracy," therefore, is decidedly inferior to the definition of what it means to be a free people with a constitutional form of government as outlined by our Declaration of Independence and Constitution.

5. The right to bear arms. The Second Amendment to our Constitution protects our inherent right of self-defense by means of bearing arms. The CCE document on "essential elements" of democracy never mentions this fundamental right. The right to bear arms is out of sight and out of mind—not surprising since the *National Standards For Civics And Government*, written by the CCE, similarly omits the right to bear arms. [See the author's *Fed Ed: The New Federal Curriculum and How It's Enforced* (St. Paul: EdWatch.org) 2002]

6. Powers reserved to the people. The Tenth Amendment to our Constitution clarifies that those rights not delegated to the federal government are reserved for the states or the people respectively. These undesignated rights are commonly known as the "reserved powers" or "reserved rights." The principle of reserved rights recognizes that the people have numerous rights not mentioned in the Constitution. Since these basic rights are inherent in the citizens and are not granted by government, it follows that any rights not specifically designated to the government by the Constitution still belong to the people. Reserved rights and inherent rights are two sides of the same coin. Neither reserved rights nor inherent rights are recognized by the CCE's description of what it calls "essential elements" of democracy.

The principles of freedom that the CCE omits are not the only cause for concern. Equally troublesome are the positions the CCE promotes in their stead. Following are two of the ideas advocated by the CCE in this article:

Promotion of the UN Declaration of the Rights of the Child. On page 6 of the article, the CCE states:

> Parents...and national governments recognize the rights of the child...in accord with the principles of the United Nations Declaration of the Rights of the Child.

The UN Declaration of the Rights of the Child is a radical document. It says, for example, that parents may not impose their religious beliefs on their children. It alleges that spanking is child abuse. The United Nations is now putting pressure on Canada to make laws making spanking illegal on the grounds that Canada has agreed to the UN Declaration of the Rights of the Child.

The obvious right of parents to govern their children is abrogated by the UN Declaration of the Rights of the Child and the CCE's view of democracy. The rights of parents are among the many reserved rights under our Constitution. If one doesn't accept the reserved powers doctrine, then the fundamental rights of parents, and numerous other rights, are vulnerable.

Promotion of the Universal Declaration of Human Rights. The CCE article also says: "These [fundamental] rights may be [explained by]...the Universal Declaration of Human Rights ..." This UN document, however, clarifies its view of human rights when it states: "These rights and freedoms may in no case be exercised contrary to the purposes and principles of the United Nations." That is, the decisions of government in general, and the policies of the UN in particular, take priority over our basic human rights. Rights that have lower standing than government policies do not amount to very much. It should also be noted that this view—that government policies have higher standing than human rights—is the same view of rights that is recognized by Communist governments.

What, then, should we make of this strategy by the CCE and others to focus on "essential elements of democracy" instead of focusing on the principles of freedom which established the foundation of government in the United States? The CCE's viewpoint is clearly inferior to that of our own founding documents. Why should we ignore our own system of freedom and look elsewhere? The reason is this—the foundational principles of freedom which established the United States, and are also the pillars of freedom available to any and all countries of the world, must be undermined by the radicals in order to create their utopian dream world of one-world government.

The GLOBE Program

By Allen Quist

Just as its name suggests, the GLOBE Program is part of an effort to establish a global system of education. Also as its name suggests, the GLOBE program looks at the world from global perspective, not from the perspective of the United States.

GLOBE is popular in the United States. There are now 10,350 U.S. schools that participate in the GLOBE program. Additional schools are signing up on a steady basis.

"GLOBE" is an acronym for "Global Learning and Observation to Benefit the Environment." That is, GLOBE is an international education system with an international curriculum and an international data collection network. The National Science Foundation (NSF) defines GLOBE as follows:

> Global Learning and Observation to Benefit the Environment (GLOBE) – [is] an international program designed to develop links between scientists and school children through a global information network. [http://www.geo.nsf.gov/adgeo/education.htm]

As clarified by its full name, the purpose of GLOBE is both international education and environmental education. A 1996 bulletin published by GLOBE highlighted these two purposes as it announced the formation of a partnership between GLOBE and UNESCO (the education arm of the United Nations). The headline read, "GLOBE-UNESCO to Work Together on Environmental Education." The article said:

> UNESCO and GLOBE will work together as appropriate toward diffusion to schools of key messages concerning

sustainable development, enhancement of teacher training with regard to education for sustainable development, and involvement of other United Nations bodies in the implementation of the Globe Program worldwide. [http://www.globe.gov/fsl/GB/Display.pl]

What do GLOBE and UNESCO mean by "diffusion to schools of key messages of sustainable development"? The "key messages of sustainable development" are defined by the Earth Charter, a document which has been officially endorsed by UNESCO and is supported by GLOBE. The Earth Charter [www.earthcharter.org] includes the following positions, or "messages" as being among what it calls its "principles" for action:

1. Earth worship (pantheism).
2. Evolution, broadly defined.
3. Socialized medicine.
4. World government.
5. Animal rights (animals are seen as our brothers and sisters).
6. Income redistribution among nations and within nations.
7. Eradication of genetically modified (GMO) crops.
8. Contraception and "reproductive health" (legal abortion).
9. World-wide "education for sustainability" which includes spiritual education.
10. Debt forgiveness for third-world nations.
11. Adoption of the gay rights agenda.
12. Elimination of nuclear weapons and elimination of the right to bear arms.
13. Redefining the media so it will support the environmental agenda, not report on it.
14. Setting aside biosphere reserves where no human presence is allowed.

As is obvious from the 14 points above, "the key messages of sustainable development" as defined by the Earth Charter include a broad religious, ideological and political agenda. How does the Earth Charter hope to accomplish its ambitious goals as defined by the Charter? The Earth Charter webpage answers that question by saying:

Education is **the key** to advancing the transition to more sustainable ways of living. **Transformative education** is needed:...The Earth Charter provides a unique framework for developing educational programs and curricula aimed at **transformative learning** for a more just, sustainable and peaceful world. [www.earthcharter.org, emphasis added]

Notice that the Earth Carter does not say that education is "**a key**" to sustainable development; the Charter says that education is "**the key**" to sustainable development. As stated above in the Earth Charter, and as also stated in various UN agreements including Agenda 21, the Treaty on Biodiversity, and Education for All, UNESCO sees **education for sustainable** development as being **the primary method** for advancing the goals of the Earth Charter as stated above.

It is obvious, therefore, that UNESCO is using its partnership with the international GLOBE Program as a means for accomplishing the radical objectives of the Earth Charter. Schools that participate in the GLOBE curriculum should expect the broad religious, ideological and political agenda of the Earth Charter to be aggressively promoted in their schools.

UNESCO has clarified that environmental education, as it sees it, is not primarily academic. In its "International Implementation Scheme" for its coming "Decade of Education for Sustainable Development," for example, UNESCO said:

> Thus, education **is the primary agent** of **transformation** toward **sustainable development**...The international community now strongly believes that we need to foster— through education—the values, behavior and lifestyles required for a sustainable future. [p. 4 of the Draft Statement, emphasis added]

That is, according to UNESCO, education for sustainable development is "transformational" education—education that focuses more on values, behavior and lifestyles than on teaching academic knowledge and skills. By means of its partnership with UNESCO, GLOBE has clarified that it sees environmental education in a manner consistent with the position of UNESCO.

How, then, does the GLOBE Program go about promoting the agenda of The Earth Charter? On its webpage, GLOBE says that its curriculum is consistent with the National Science Education Standards and the National Geography Standards. These national standards are transformational in nature, just as UNESCO says they should be. Like The Earth Charter, they focus on attitudes, values and behavior as opposed to emphasizing academic education. The National Geography

Standards, for example, do not require that students learn the l[c]
of the nations of the world, nor are students required to learn th[e]
tals of the nations. These standards do not even require that st[u]
learn the location of our 50 states and their capitals.

What, then, do the National Geography Standards require th[at]
dents know? Following the format of transformational educatio[n]
geography standards are organized around themes, not knowledge
themes are of two types—sustainable development themes and, to a
extent, multiculturalism. There are, for example, numerous requirem[ents]
for promoting sustainable development themes such as the followin[g]

> Analyze the role of people in decreasing the diversity of flora
> and fauna in a region (e.g. the impact of acid rain on rivers
> and forests in Southern Ontario, the effects of toxic dumping
> on ocean ecosystems, the effects of over fishing along the
> coast of northeastern North America or the Philippine archi-
> pelago) [p. 212]

> Describe the spatial consequences of...increases in runoff and
> sediment, tropical soil degradation, habitat destruction, air
> pollution, alternations in hydrologic cycle [p. 212]

> Examine the characteristics of major global environmental
> changes...(e.g. increases in world temperatures attributable
> to major global environmental change, results of greenhouse
> effect attributable to human action...[p. 213]

> Develop contemporary and historical case studies...(e.g. the
> drought-plagued Sahel, the depleted rain forests of central
> Africa, the Great Plains Dust Bowl) [p. 214]

> Discuss how and why some countries use greater than aver-
> age amounts of resources (e.g. German iron-ore imports, and
> petroleum consumption in the United States and Japan) [p.
> 216] [The implication is that economic growth and activity is
> a mater of fairness, not an issue of following sound principles
> of economics.]

> Compare the attitudes of different religions toward the envi-
> ronment and resource use and how religions have affected
> world economic development patterns and caused cultural
> conflict or encouraged social integration [p. 219] [The

clarified by the UN's Treaty on Biodiversity,
nity is supposedly harmful to the environment
hes that man is above the rest of nature, while
upposedly environmentally friendly because it
are is the steward of man.]

Geography Standards are packed full of require-
above. These standards really should be called the
tion for Sustainable Development Standards" because
iey actually are. The National Science Education
arly, have numerous requirements for teaching sustain-
nt.
ee, therefore, is substantial consistency between the
;CO and the GLOBE Program. The principles of free-
by the United States, and as stated in our Declaration of
, are contrary to the purposes of GLOBE and UNESCO
be taught. National sovereignty, for example, is under-
GLOBE Program.
: purpose of UNESCO was made crystal clear by its first
:neral, Sir Julian Huxley, when he said:

cally, in its educational program it [UNESCO] can stress
imate need for world political unity and familiarize all
:s with the implications of the transfer of full sovereignty
separate nations to a world organization...political unifi-
1 in some sort of world government will be required. [Sir
1 Huxley, UNESCO: Its Purpose and Philosophy, 1947,
·]

is also the purpose of GLOBE—creating an international sys-
:ducation for sustainable development as defined by the Earth
International education is a critical step in UNESCO's overall
iternational government.